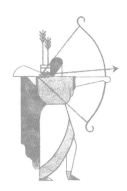

blue
rider
press

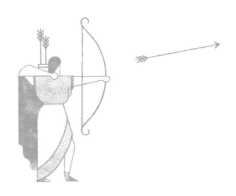

THE BOOK OF EXTRAORDINARY DEATHS
True Accounts of Ill-Fated Lives

Cecilia Ruiz

Blue Rider Press
New York

blue
rider
press

An imprint of Penguin Random House LLC
375 Hudson Street
New York, New York 10014

ISBN 9780399184048

Printed in China
10 9 8 7 6 5 4 3 2 1

BOOK DESIGN BY CECILIA RUIZ

To my brothers

I had seen birth and death
but had thought they were different.

—T. S. Eliot

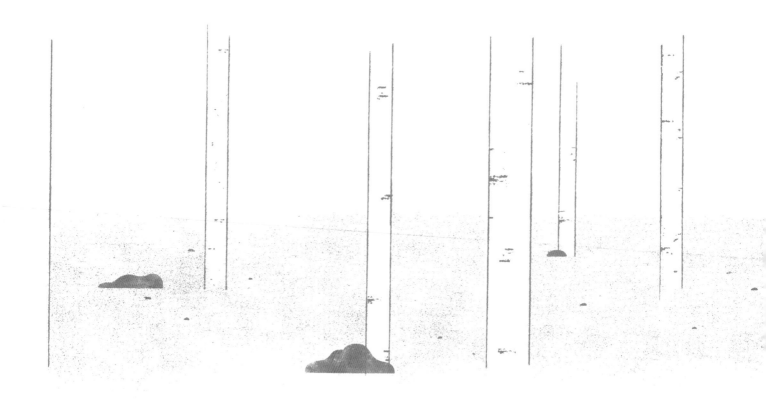

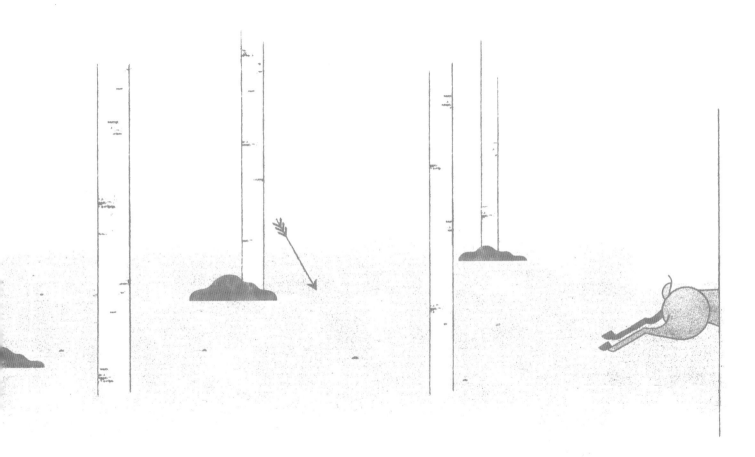

Draco

7th century BC

Following an address to the citizens of Aegina, Draco—the remarkable Athenian lawmaker—suffocated under a pile of cloaks that had been thrown to him as gifts of gratitude and admiration.

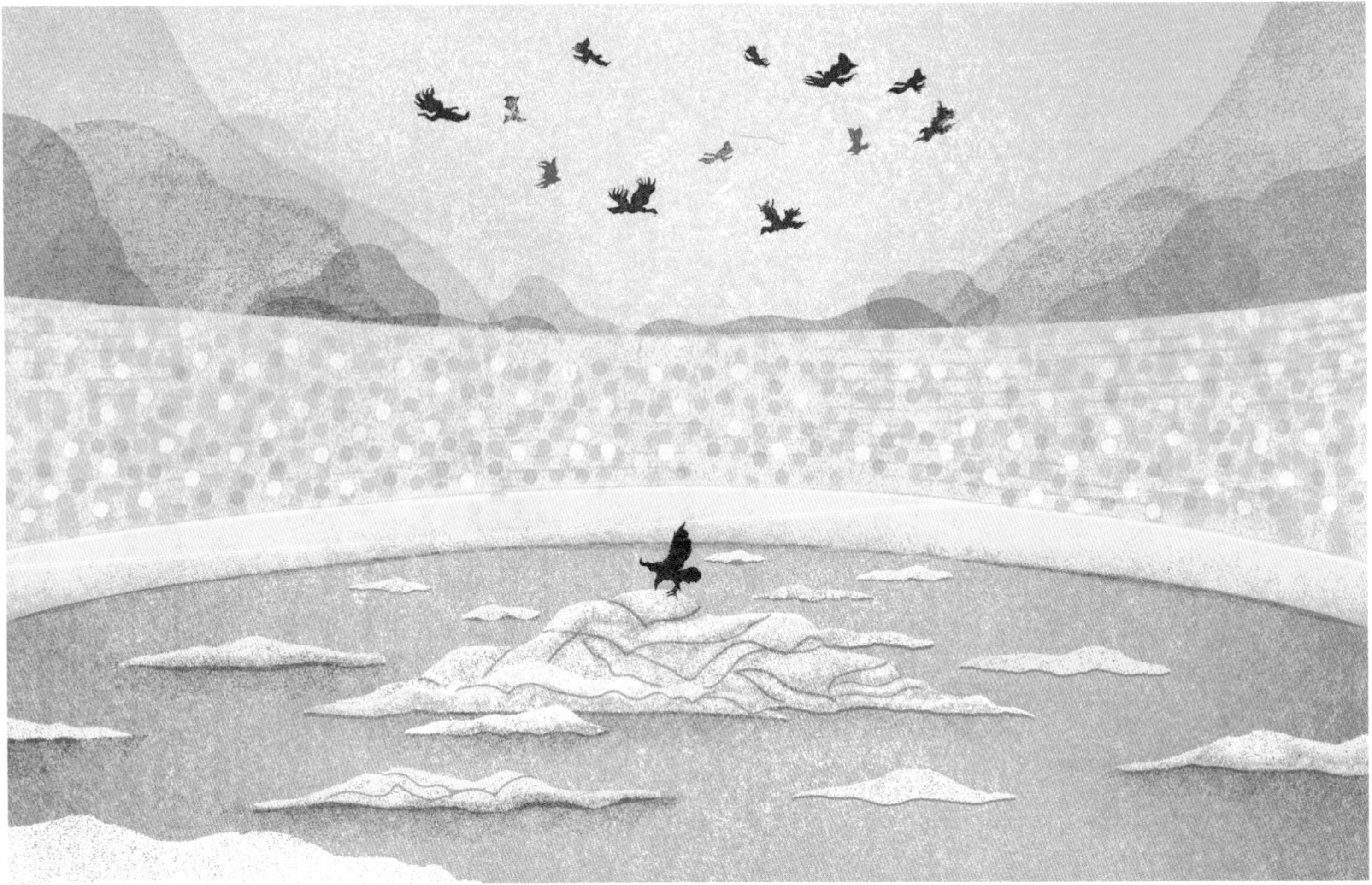

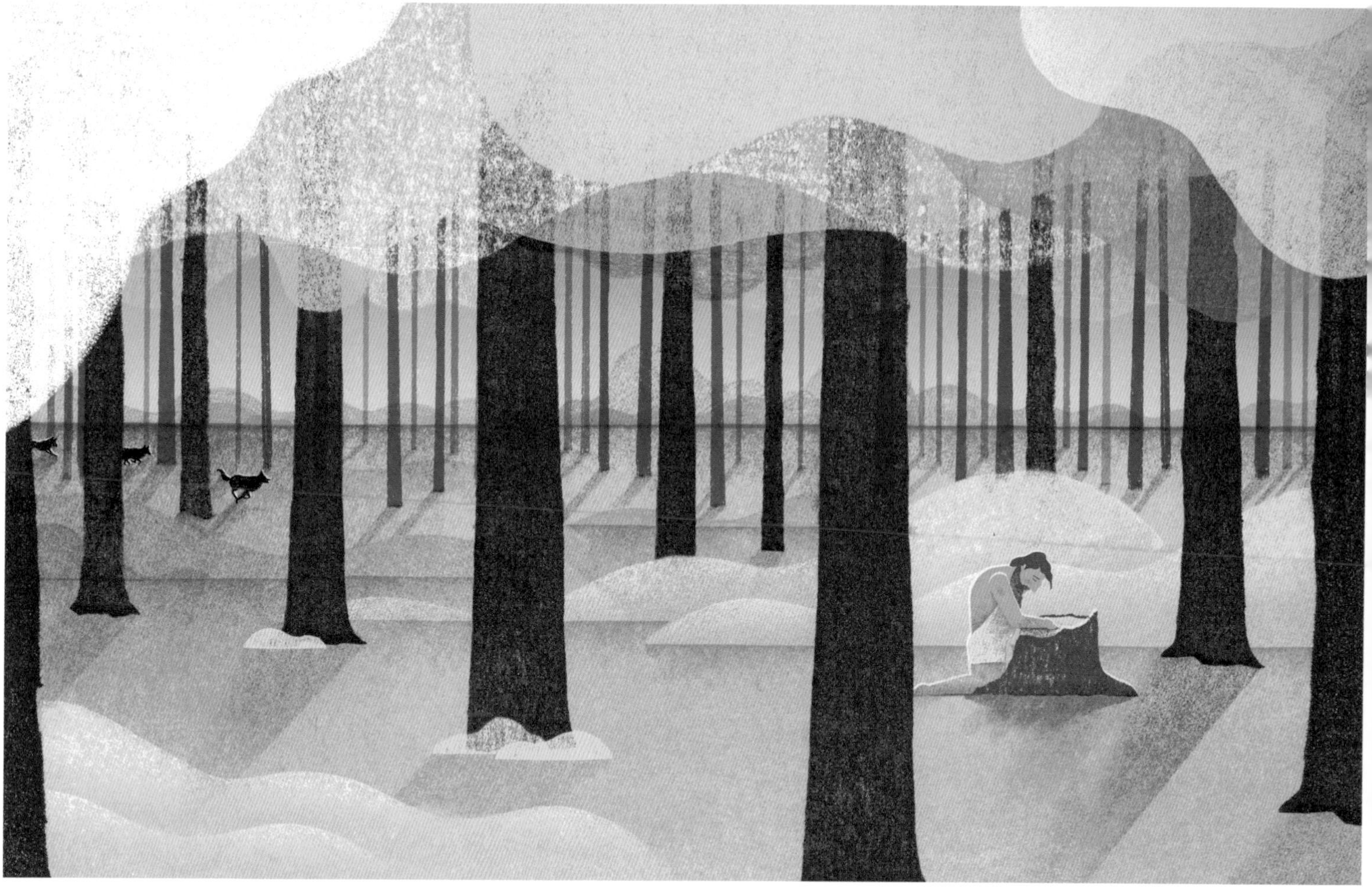

Milo of Croton
6th century BC

Milo of Croton, the notable Greek wrestler, encountered his death in the forest.
As he came upon a broken tree trunk split with wedges, he decided to test his strength by
tearing the stump in two. The wedges fell and trapped his hands in the tree trunk,
leaving him defenseless against hungry wolves.

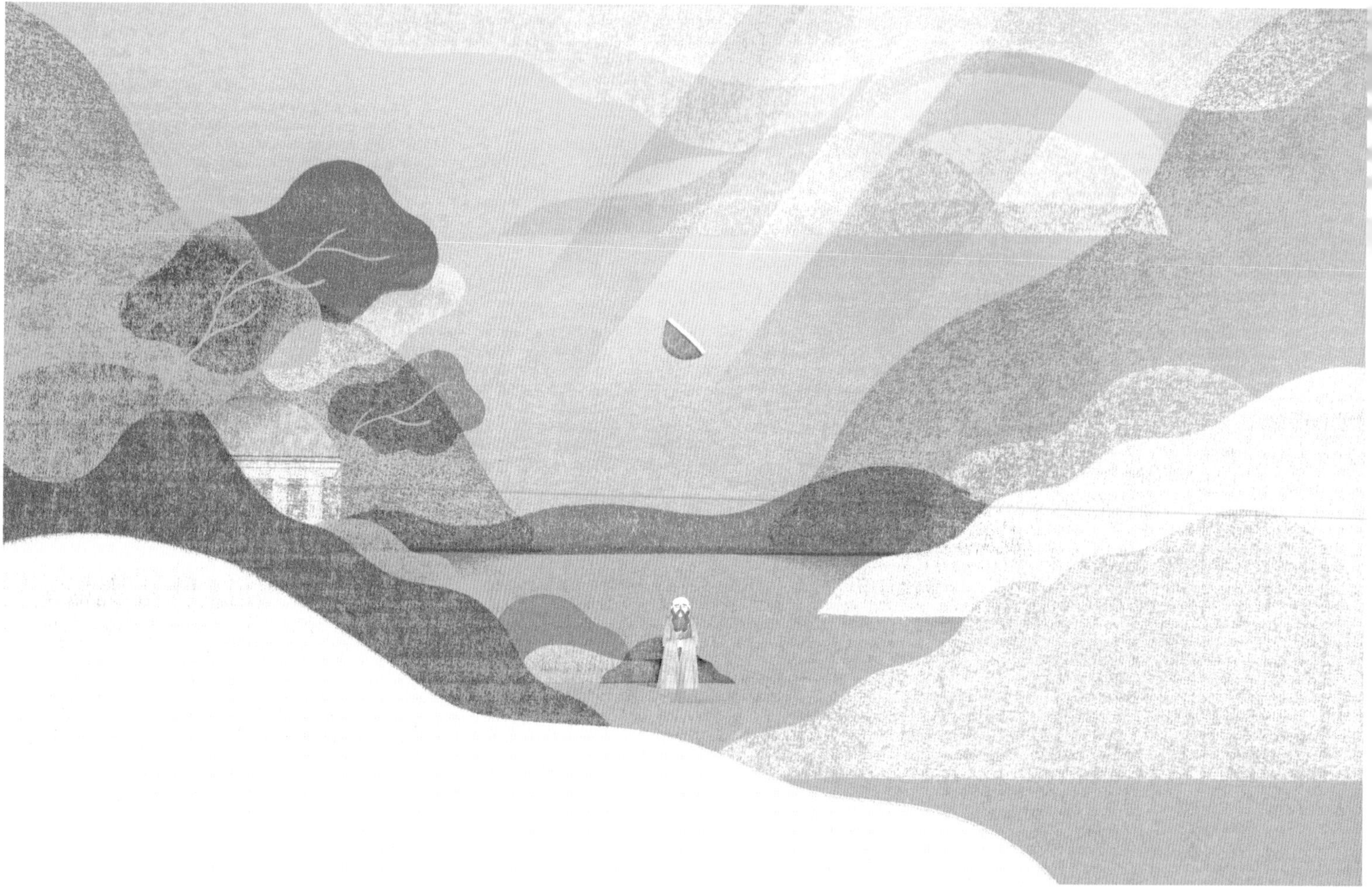

Aeschylus
5th century BC

Aeschylus, the Athenian author known as the father of Greek tragedy, died when an eagle flying high above dropped a tortoise on his head. It is believed that the passing creature may have mistaken his bald head for a rock on which to crack open the shell of the reptile.

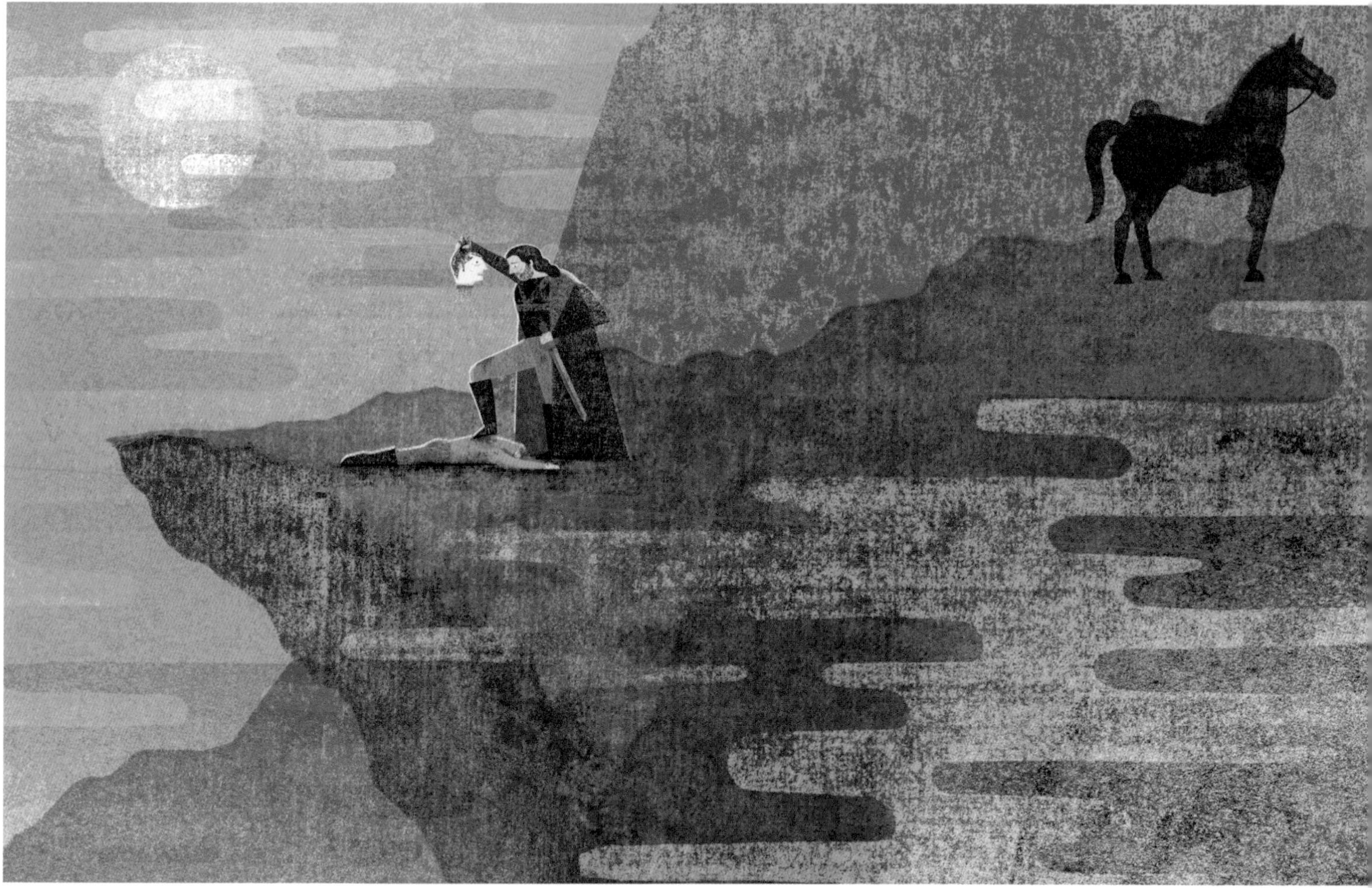

Sigurd the Mighty
892

Sigurd the Mighty was a Viking warrior from Orkney (now Scotland),
whose death was wrought by the lifeless head of nobleman Máel Brigte. After defeating and
decapitating his opponent, Sigurd strapped the head to his saddle. As he rode in victory,
the teeth in Brigte's skull scraped Sigurd's leg, causing a fatal infection.

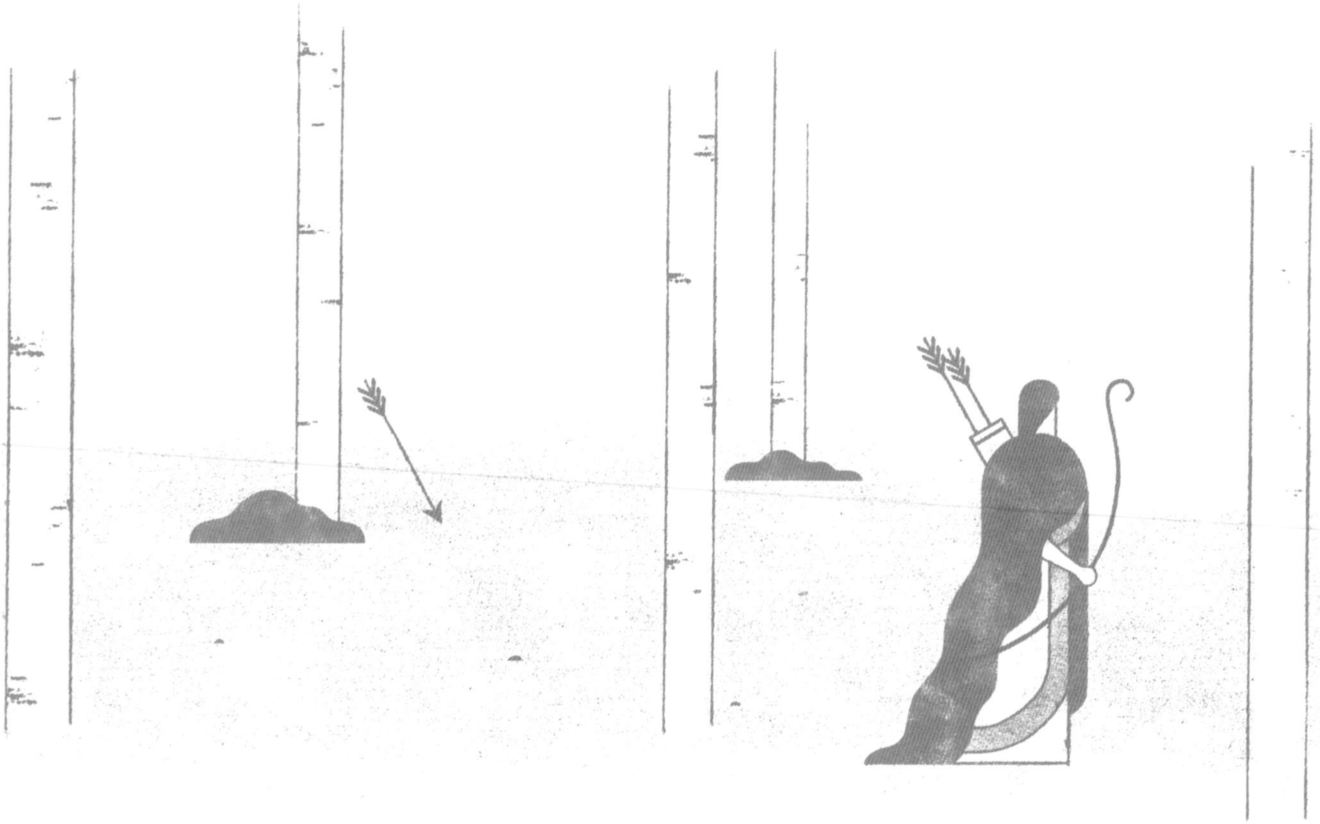

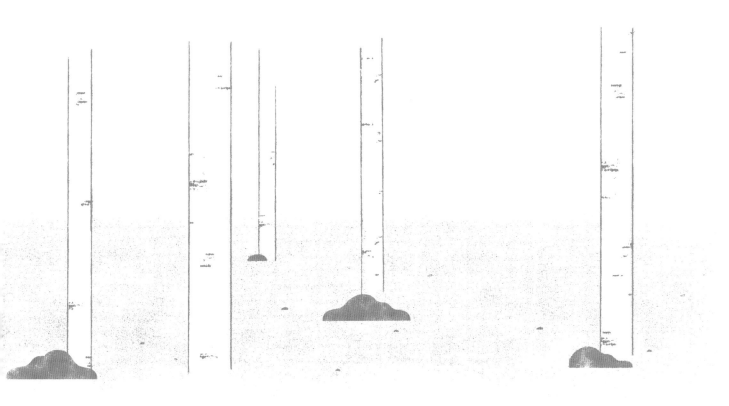

George Plantagenet
1478

It is rumored that George Plantagenet, the first Duke of Clarence, was drowned in a barrel of Malmsey wine at his own request. He had been accused and sentenced to death for plotting against his brother King Edward IV.

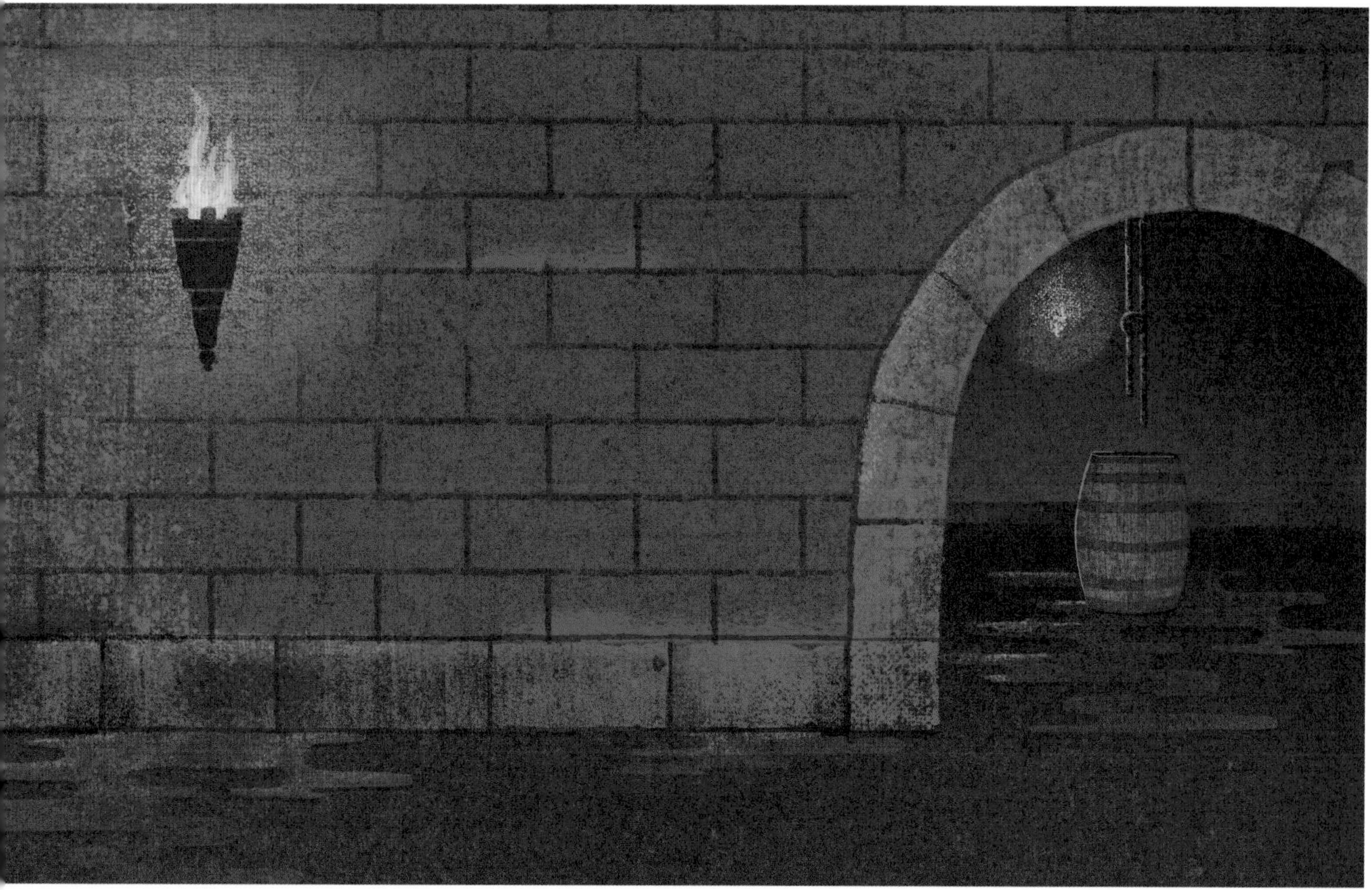

Dancing Plague
1518

In Strasbourg, Alsace, around four hundred people, for no apparent reason, gave in to dancing for days without rest. The episode lasted more than a month, in which some people died from heart attacks, strokes, or simply out of exhaustion.

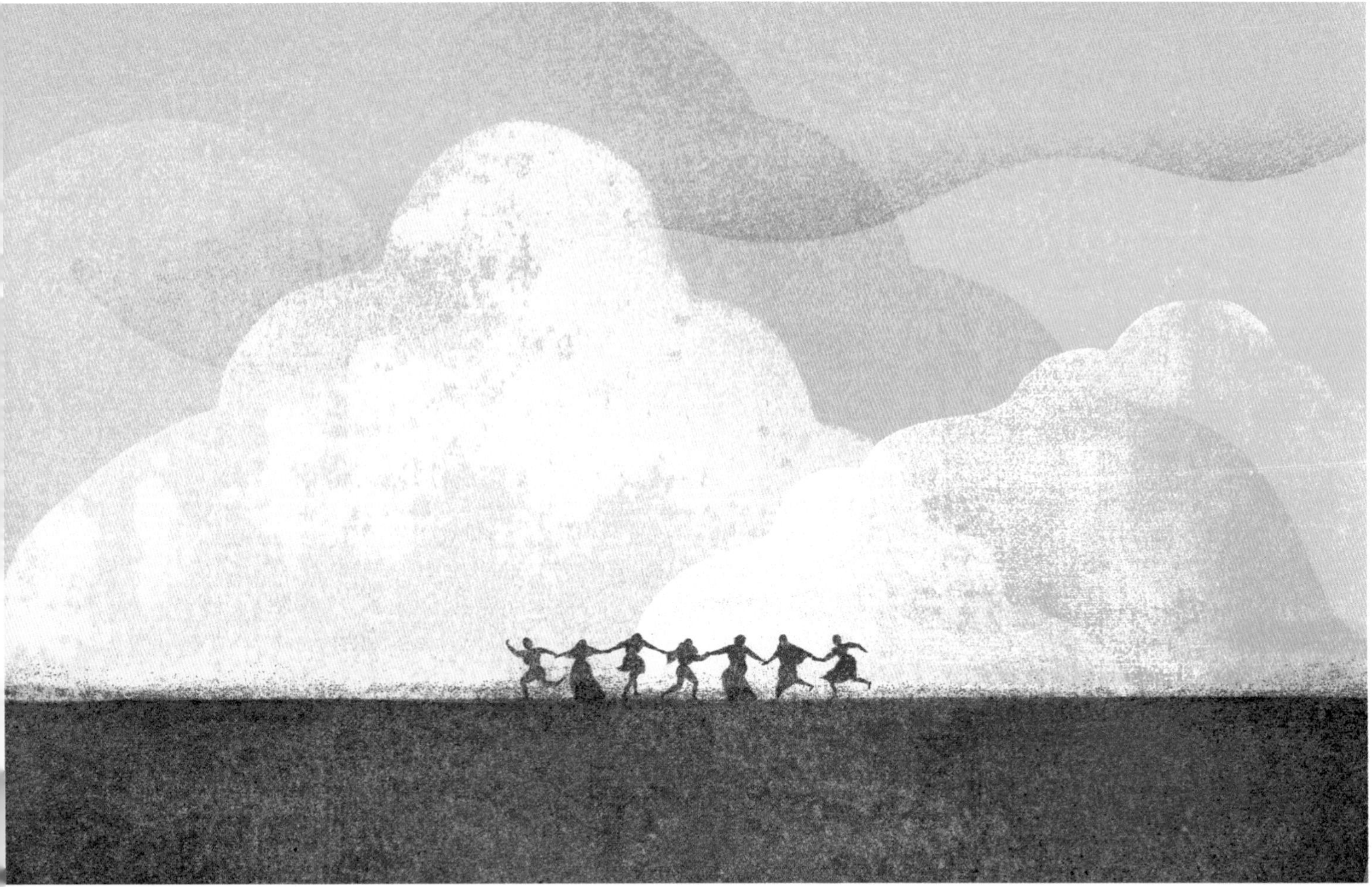

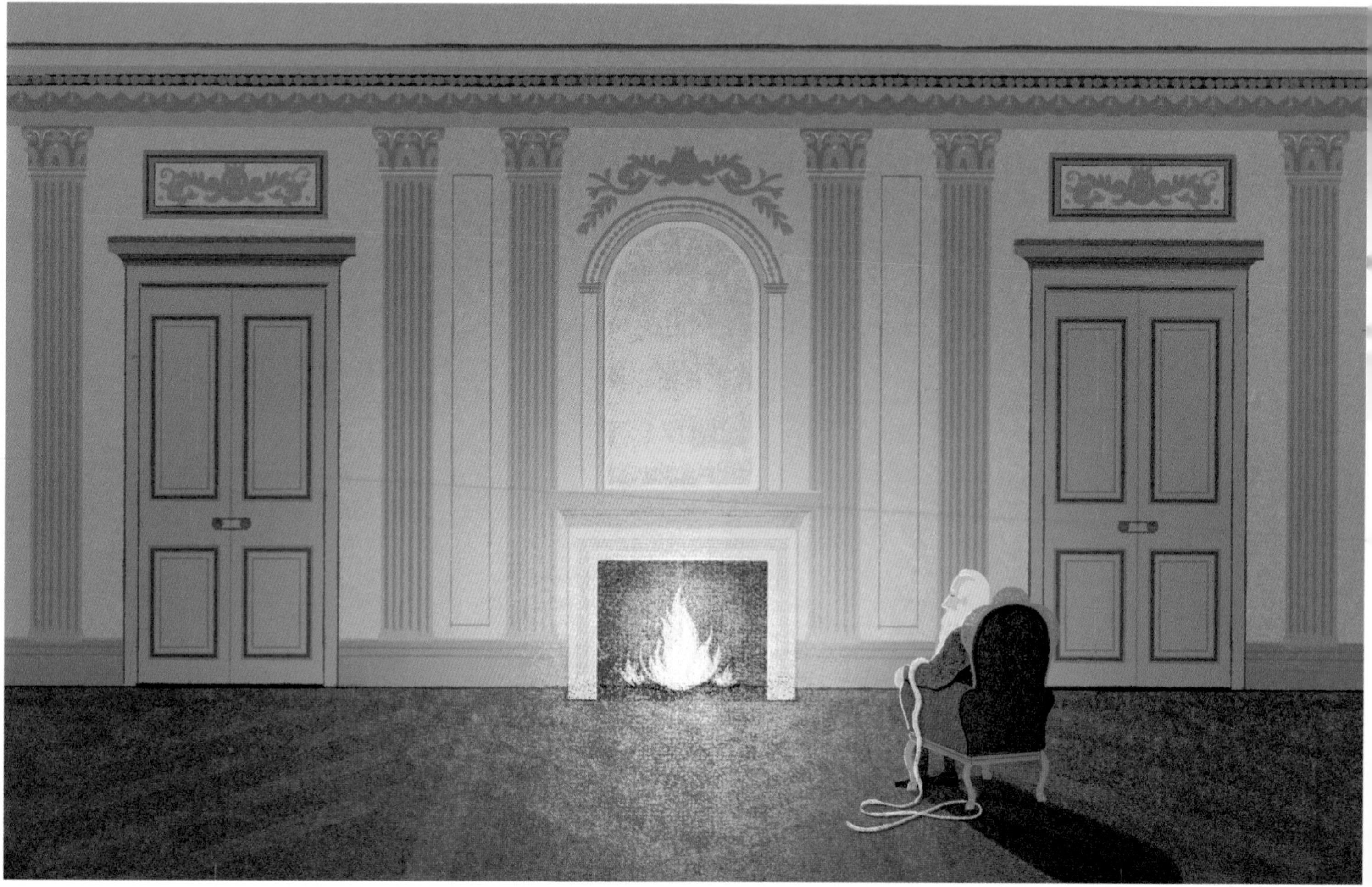

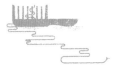

Hans Steininger

1567

Hans Steininger, the mayor of Braunau (now Austria), broke his neck when, in an attempt to escape a fire that sparked chaos in town, he tripped over his own beard. The length of his well-maintained whiskers, which he usually kept rolled up inside a leather pouch, ran from four to five feet.

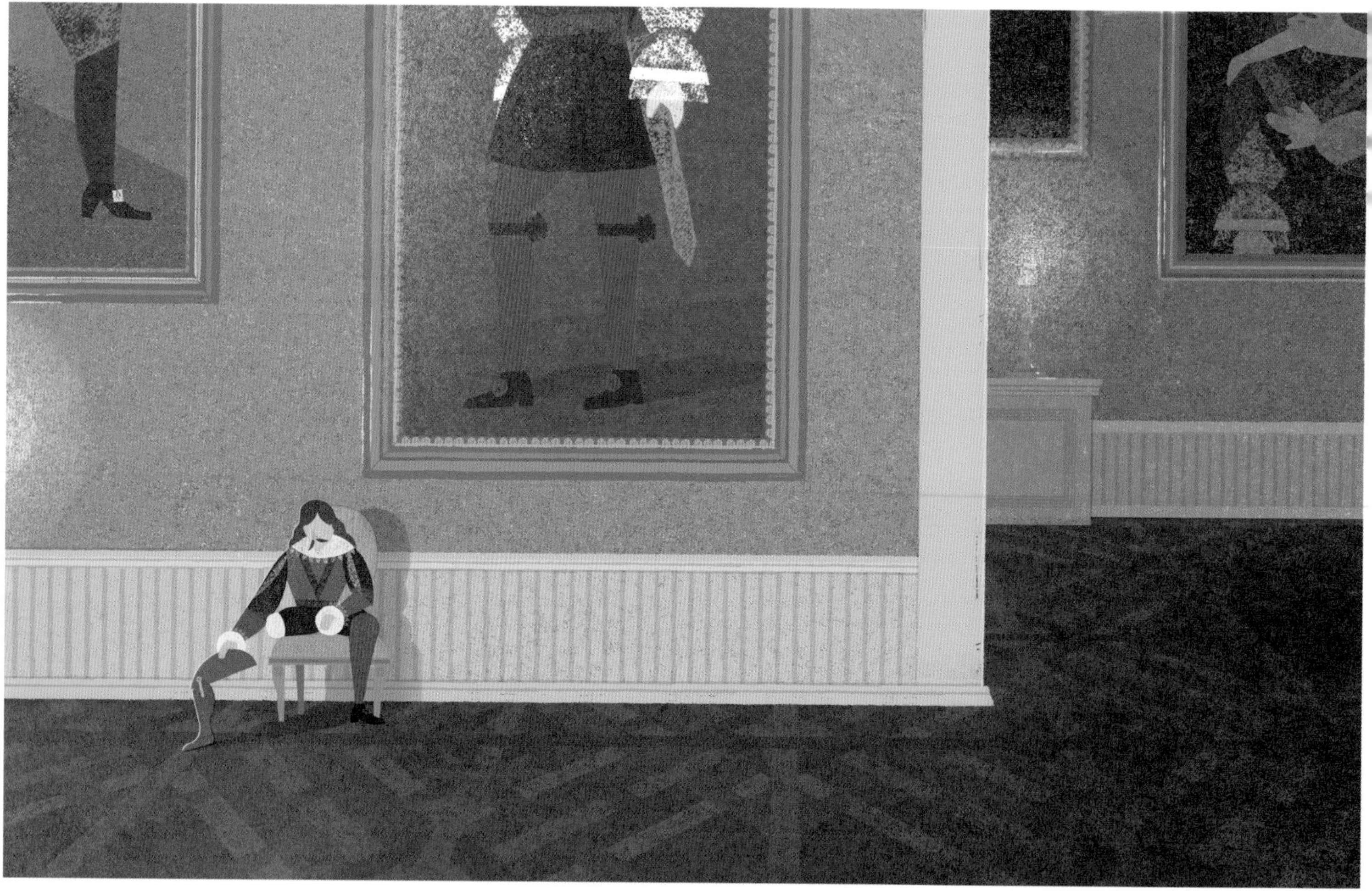

Sir Arthur Aston
1649

Sir Arthur Aston, a Royalist commander during the Siege of Drogheda, was
beaten to death with his own wooden leg by Parliamentarian soldiers.

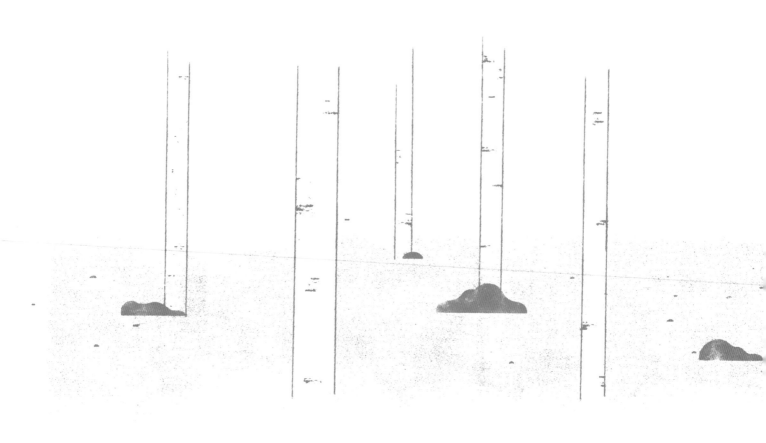

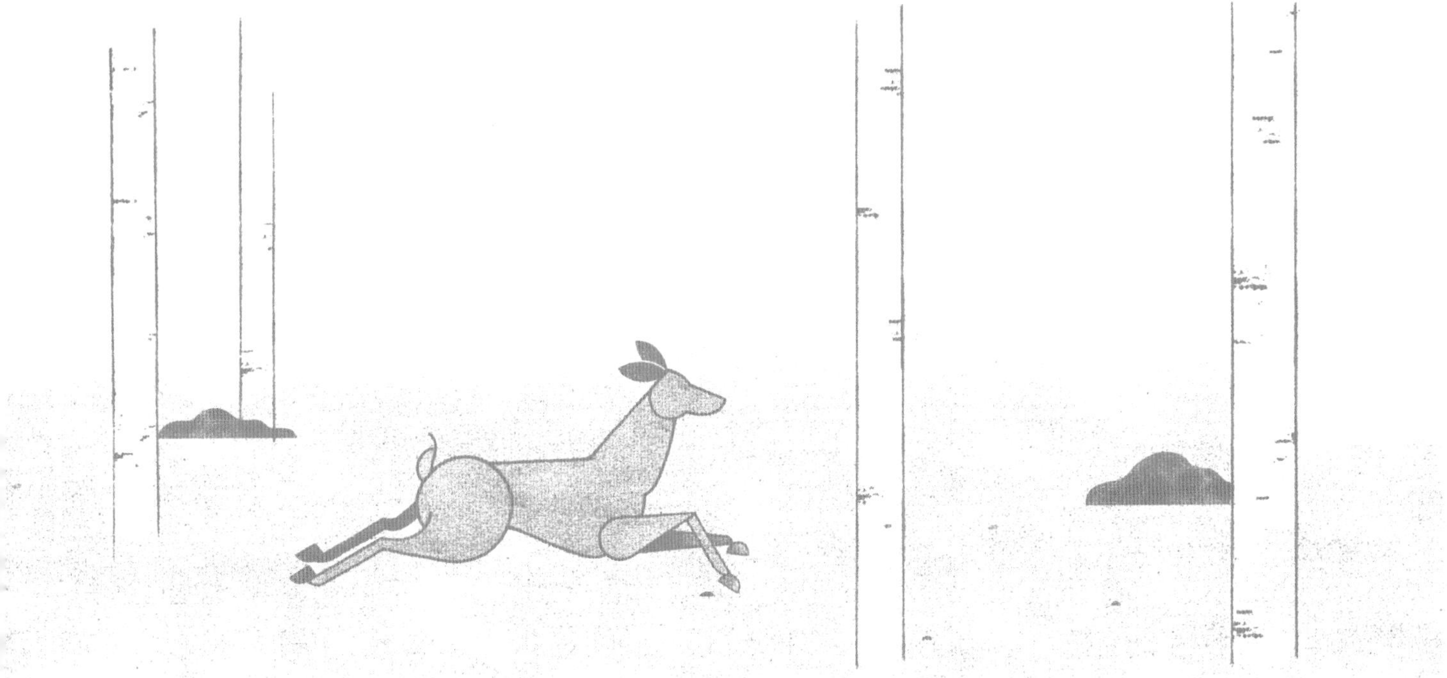

Molière

1673

Molière, the famous French playwright, perished a few hours after collapsing on stage while performing the role of a hypochondriac in his final masterpiece, *The Imaginary Invalid.*

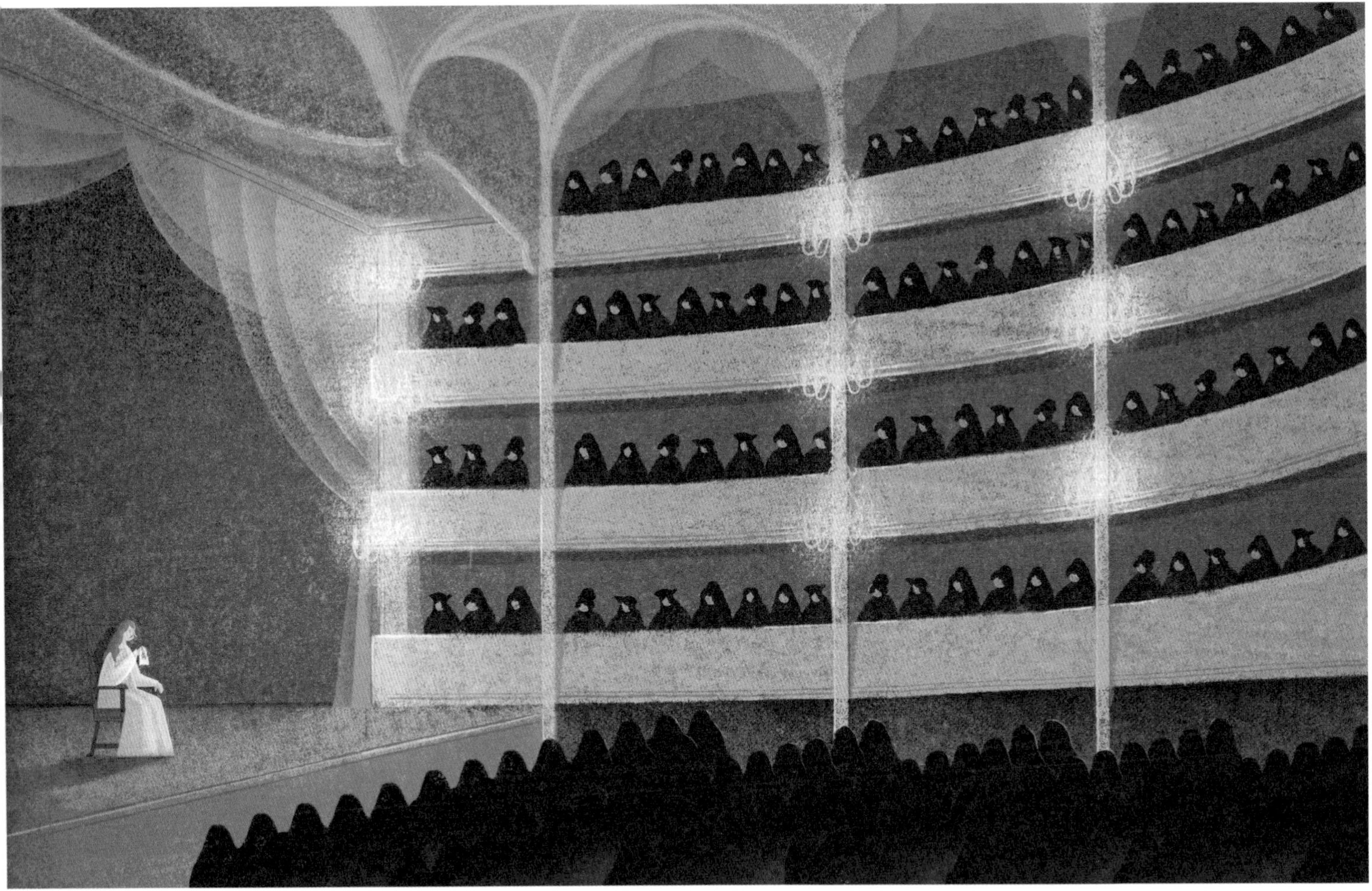

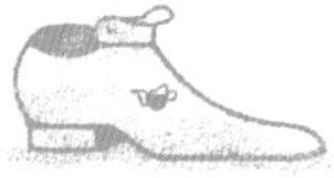

Jean-Baptiste Lully
1687

Jean-Baptiste Lully was a French composer, instrumentalist, and dancer who died from a gangrenous abscess after piercing his own foot while conducting an orchestra. Before batons were commonplace, conductors pounded the floor with staffs to keep time.

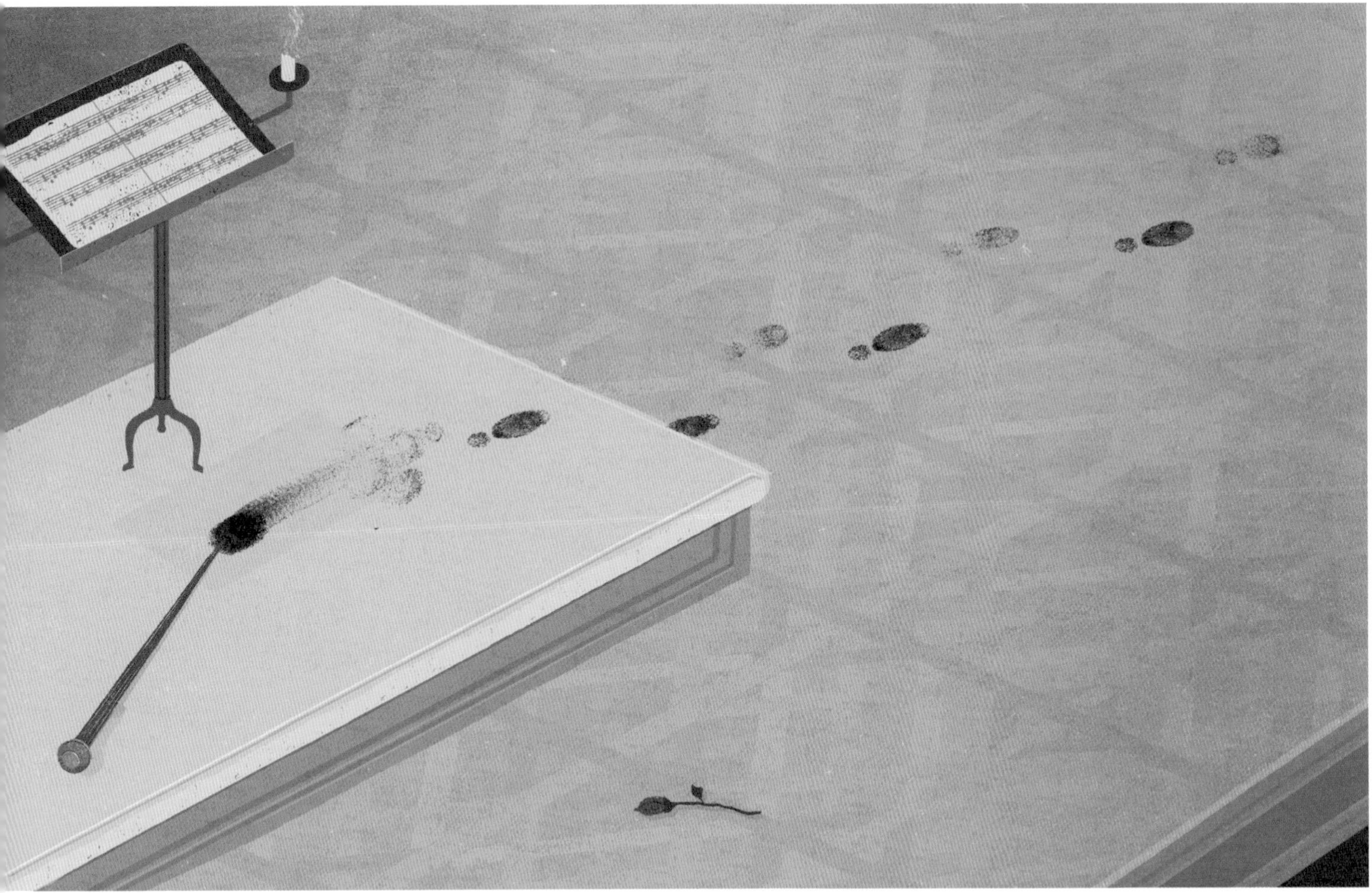

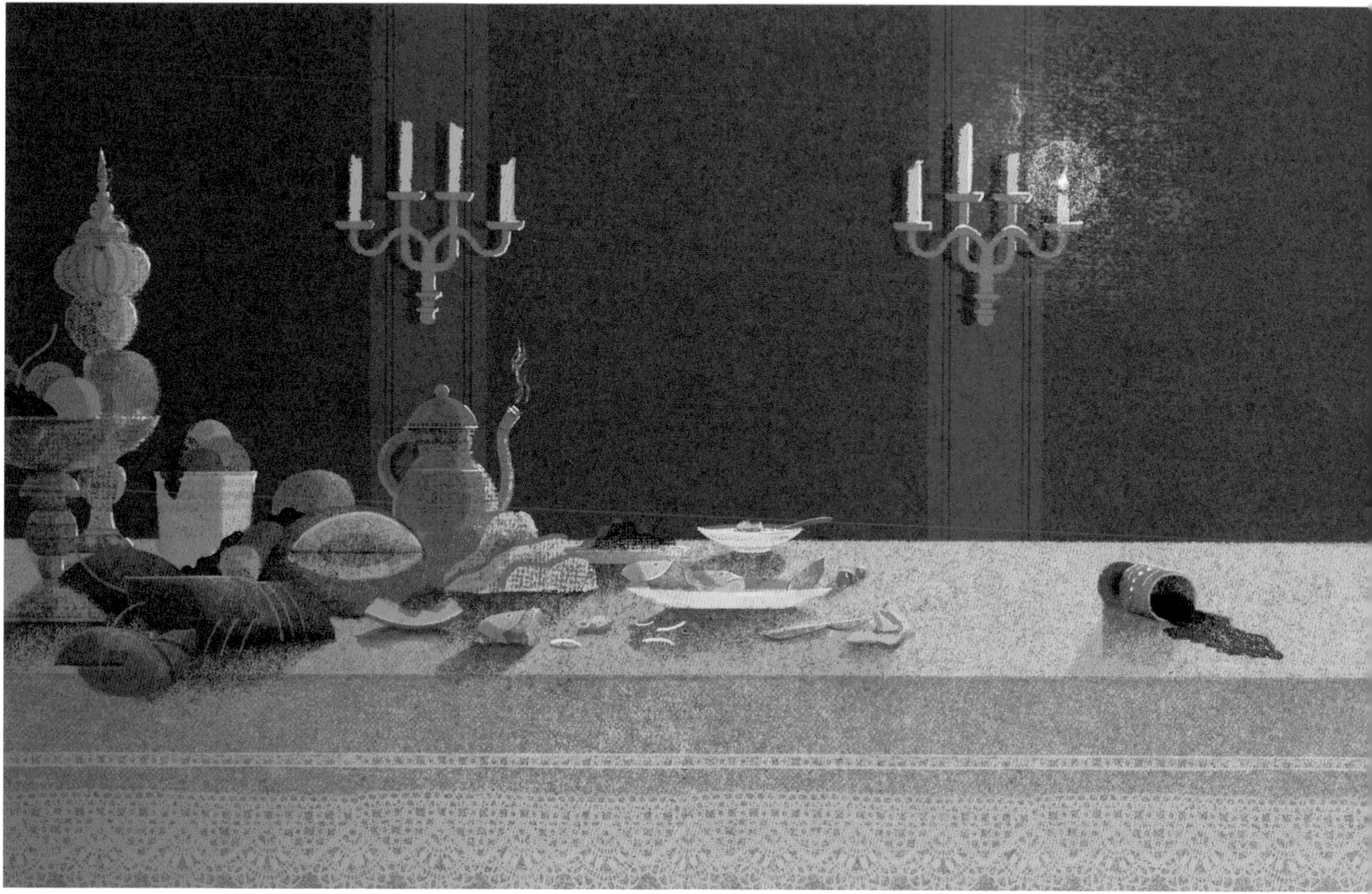

Adolf Frederick, King of Sweden
1771

Adolf Frederick is known as the king who ate himself to death. He died from digestive complications after partaking in a royal meal of lobster, caviar, sauerkraut, smoked herring, and champagne. The feast culminated with his favorite dessert, called hetvägg—a traditional Nordic dish that consists of a bread bun served in a bowl of hot milk. He had fourteen servings.

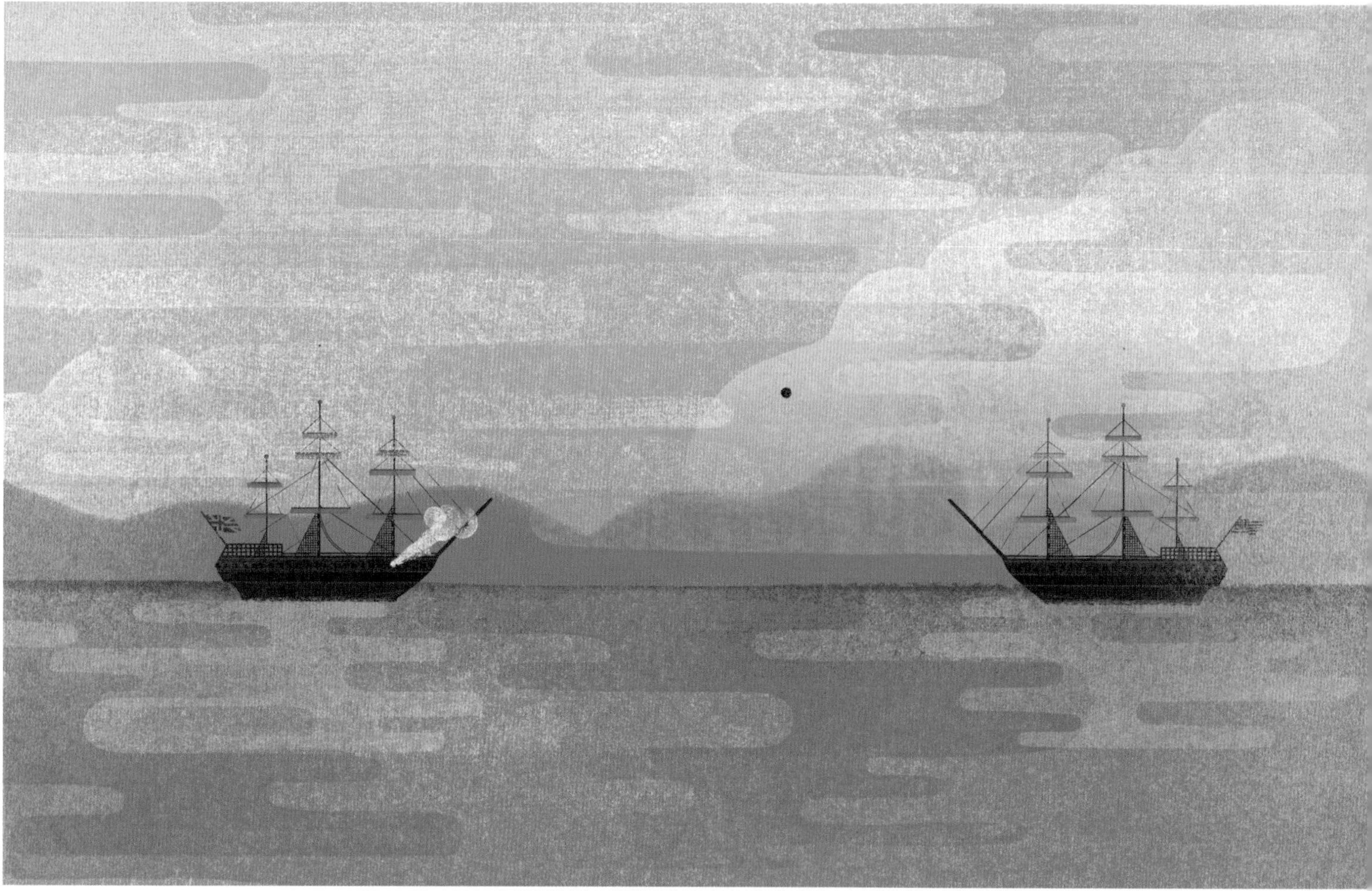

John Kendrick
1794

John Kendrick was an American sea captain who died off the coast of Honolulu
when an allied vessel fired a cannonball that was intended only to be a salute.

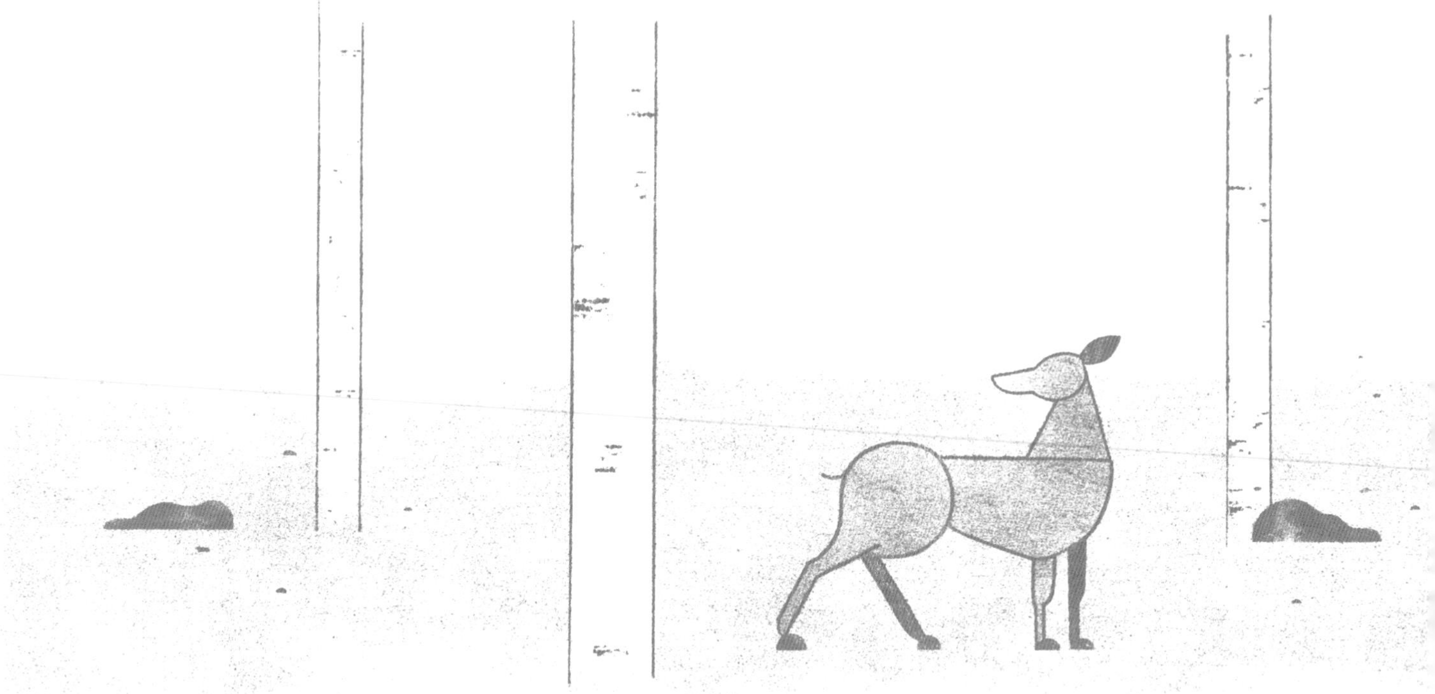

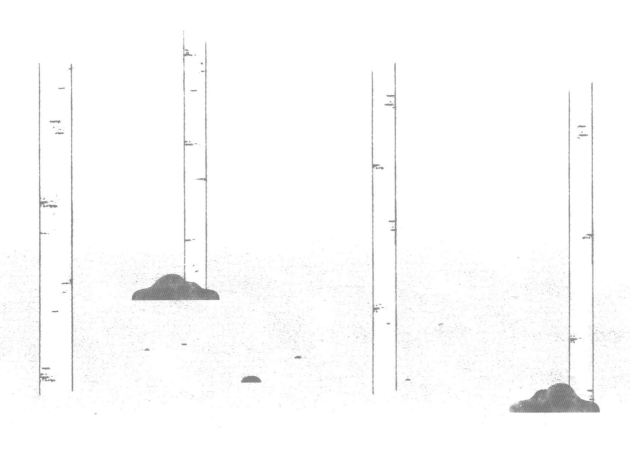

Monsieur Le Pique
1808

Monsieur Le Pique was a Frenchman who died in a duel that took place in the sky.

After an argument over a woman with his rival, Monsieur de Grandpré, the two gentlemen, who considered themselves above the rest of society, agreed that the best place to settle their dispute was among the clouds.

They ascended in hot-air balloons. Le Pique fired first but missed; Grandpré took aim and successfully struck his opponent's balloon. The aircraft plummeted to the ground, killing both Le Pique and his unfortunate second.

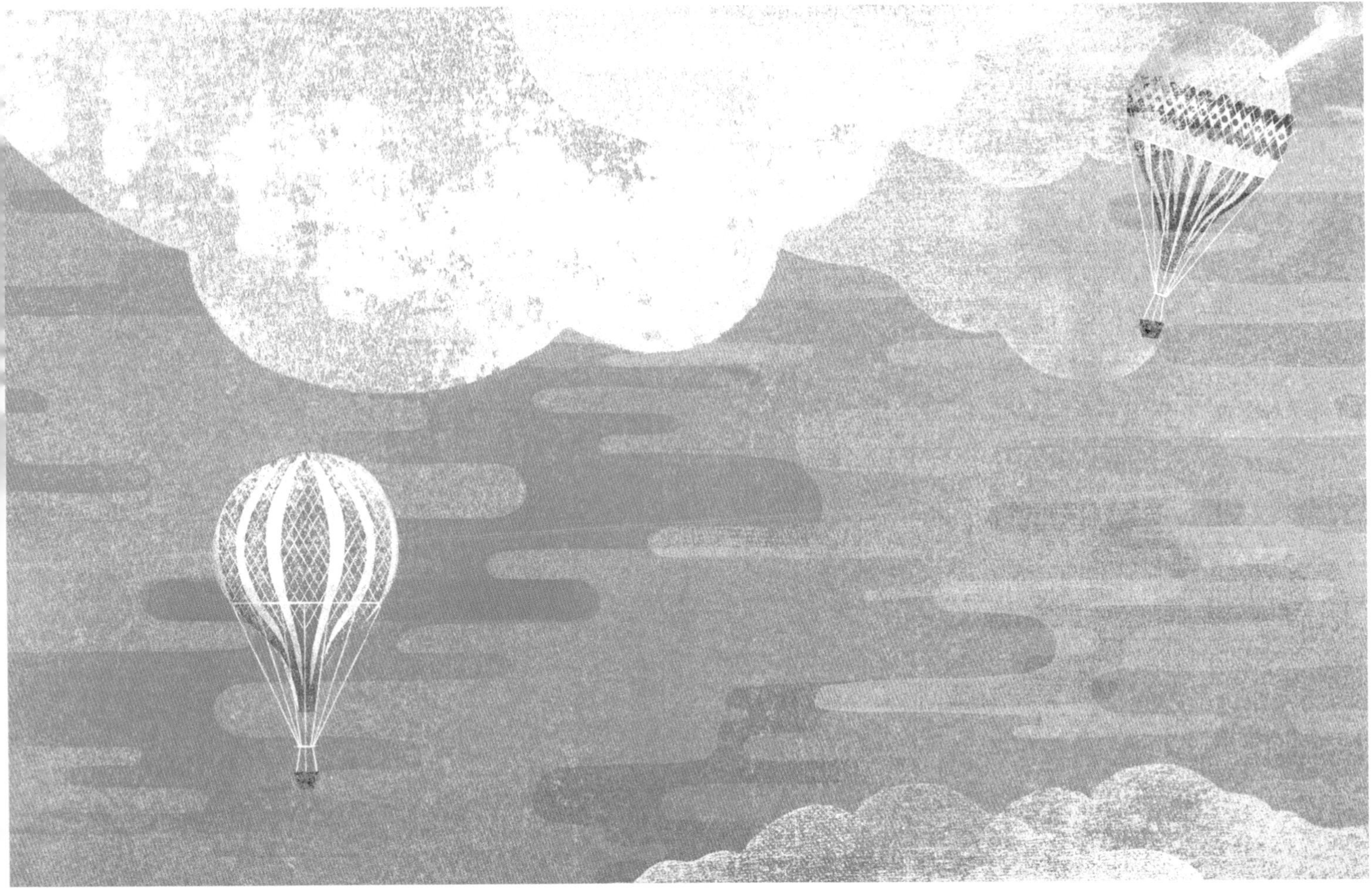

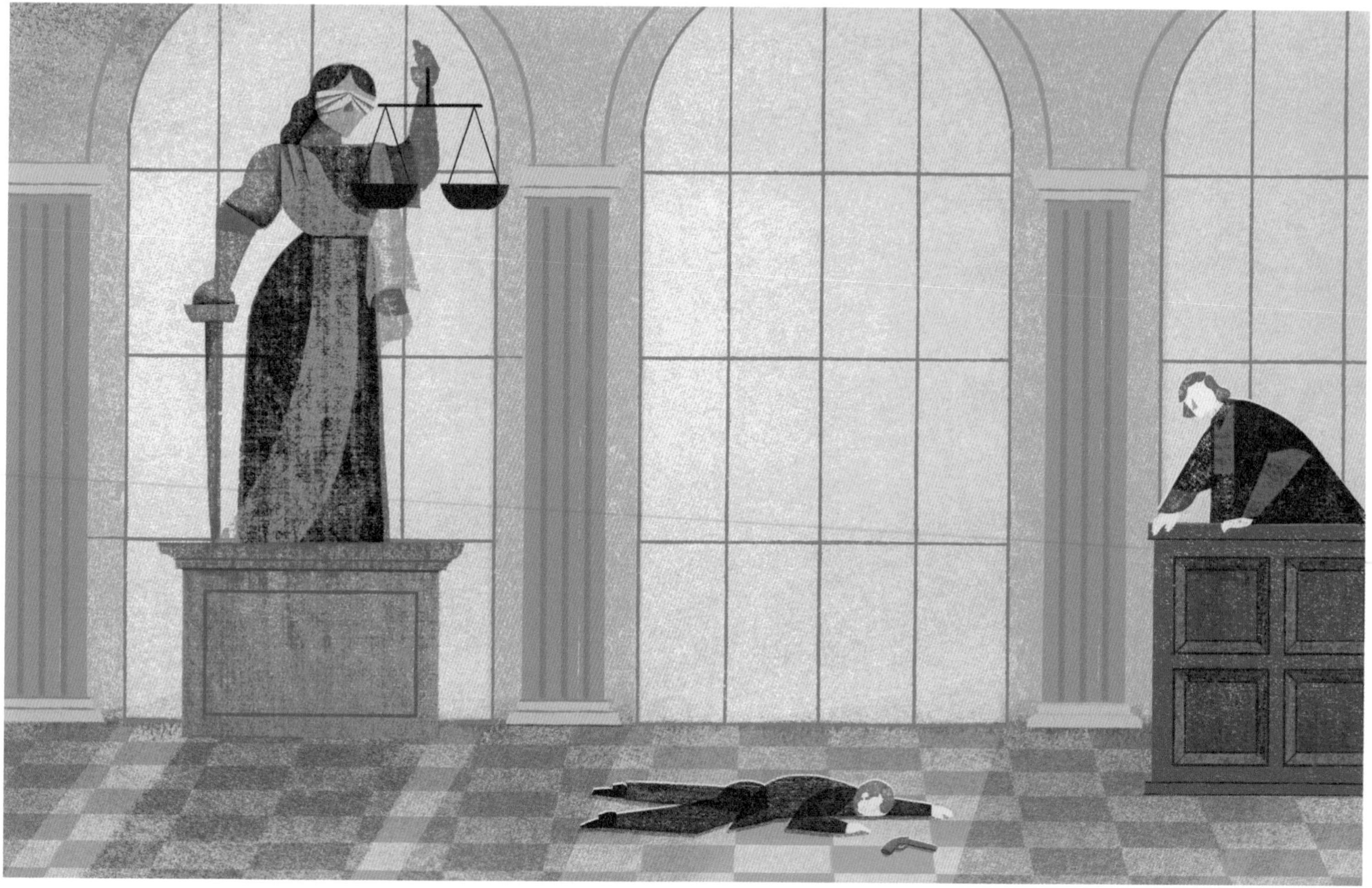

Clement Vallandigham
1871

Clement Vallandigham was an American congressman who died while defending a murder suspect on
trial. In the course of arguing that the victim could have accidentally shot himself while drawing a gun,
Vallandigham tried to prove his point by reenacting the scene. Unaware that the gun was loaded,
he accidentally shot himself and made his case.

Murderous Mary

1916

Mary, a five-ton Asian elephant, was publicly executed by hanging from an industrial crane after attacking and killing one of her trainers at the Sparks World-Famous Shows circus in Tennessee.

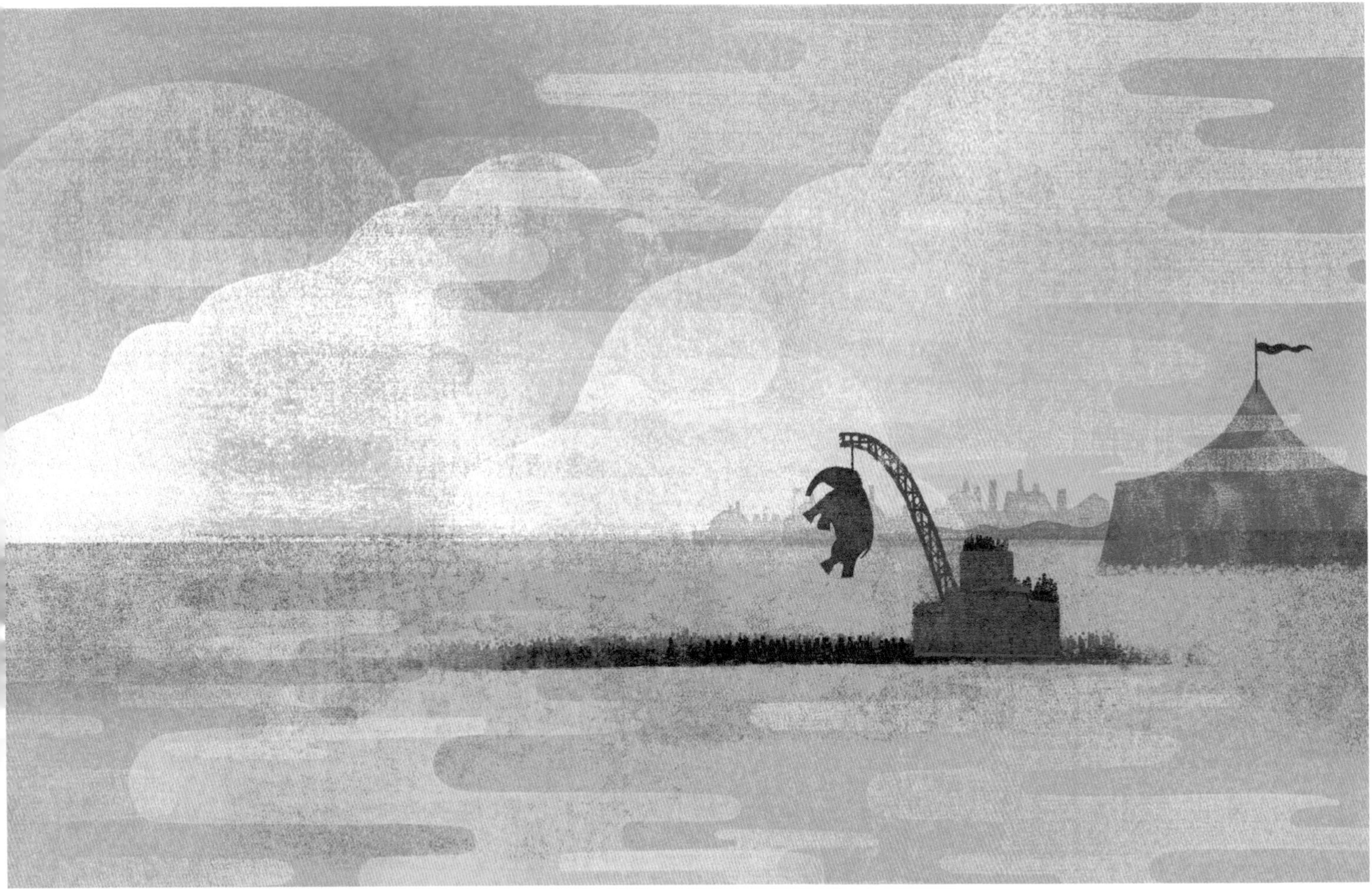

The Great Molasses Flood
1919

The darkest of floods happened in Boston.
Twenty-one people perished and hundreds were injured when a steel tank, holding
two million gallons of hot molasses, exploded and poured into the streets.

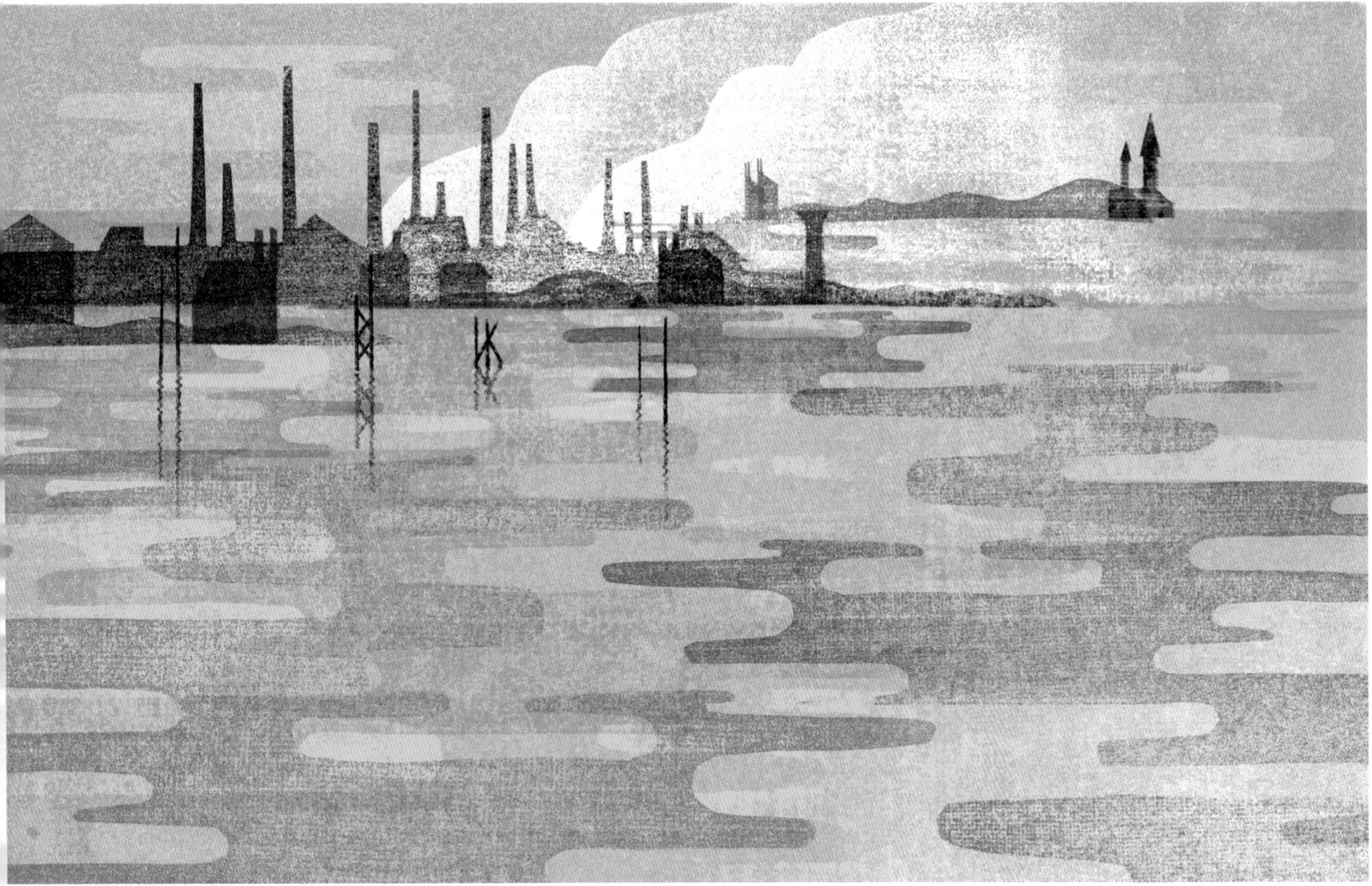

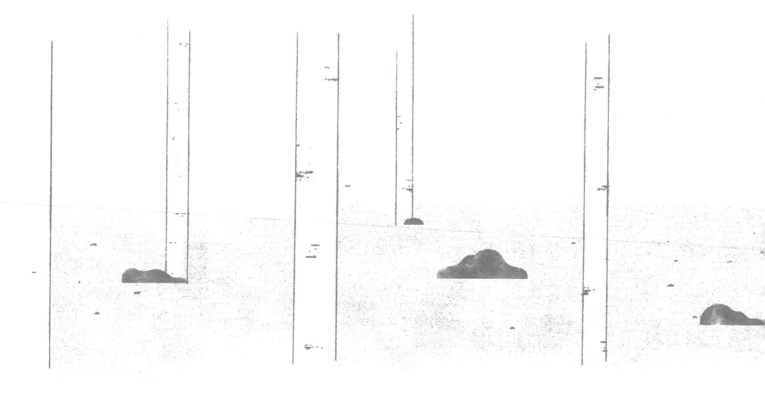

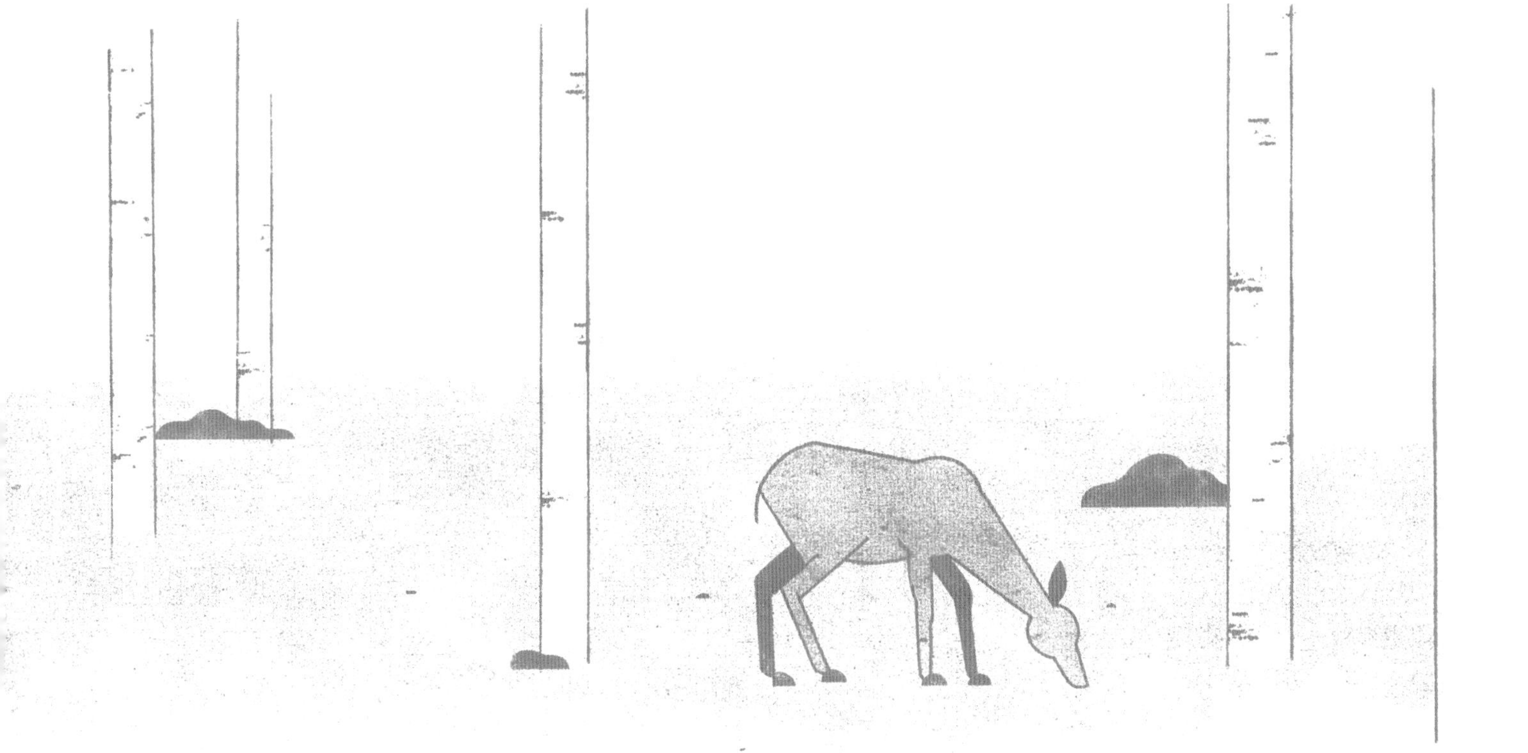

Frank Hayes

1923

Frank Hayes, a trainer-turned-jockey at Belmont Park, New York, died of a heart attack during the course of his first race. His horse, Sweet Kiss, finished in first place with Hayes's inert body still attached to the saddle. Sweet Kiss was renamed Sweet Kiss of Death and no one ever dared to ride her again.

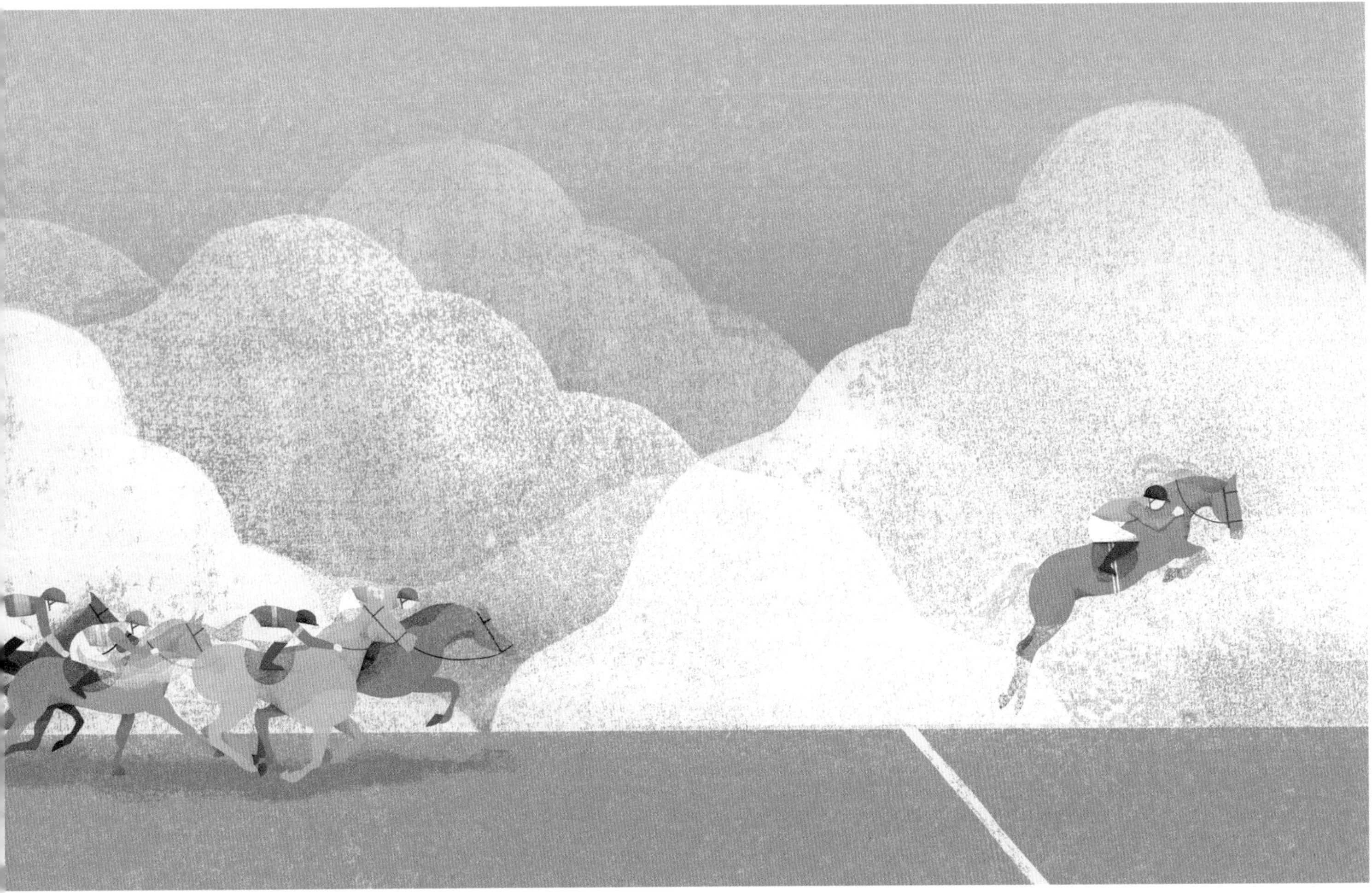

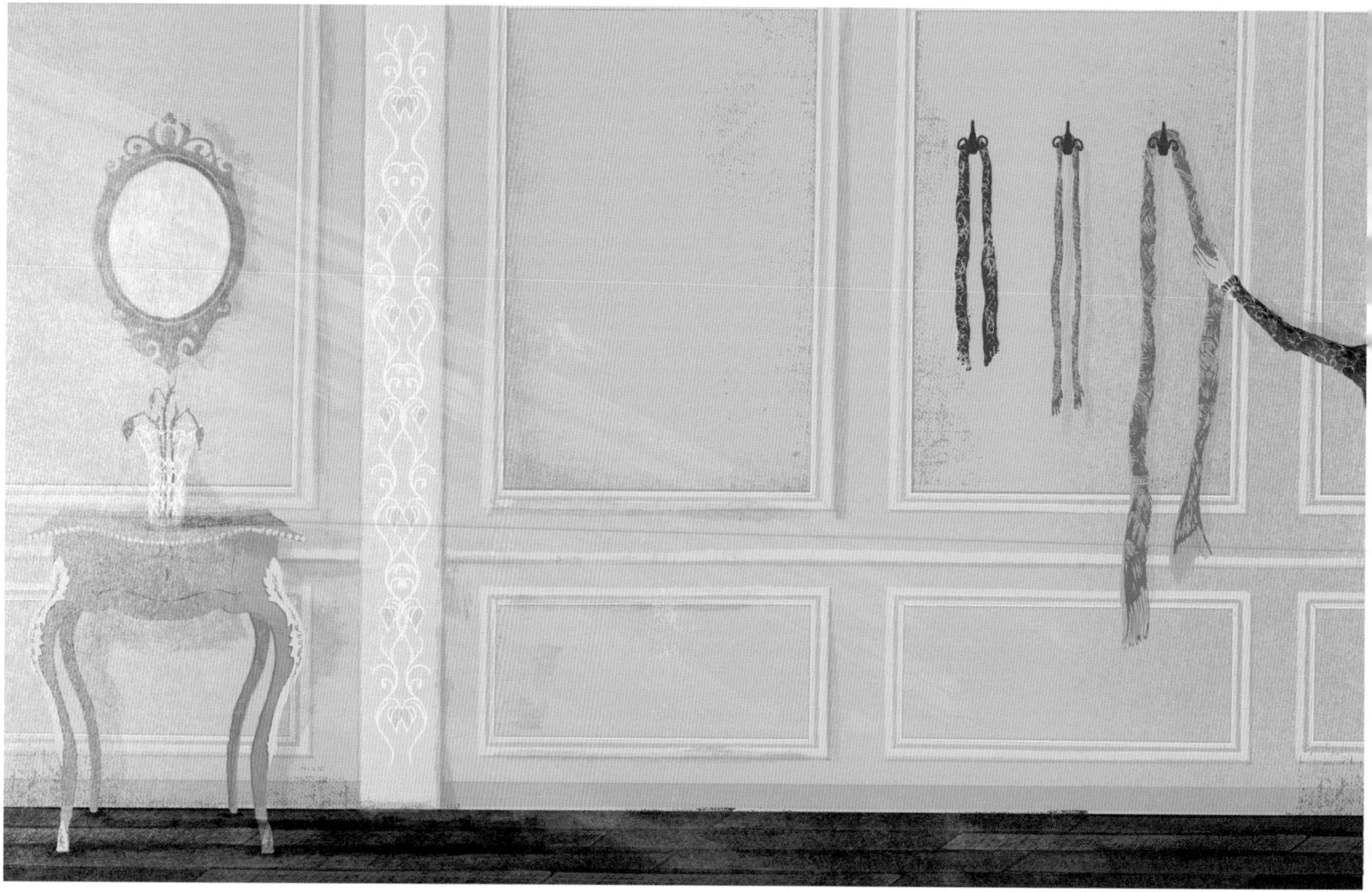

Isadora Duncan

1927

Isadora Duncan, the famous American dancer, died of a broken neck when her long scarf got caught in the wheel of an automobile in which she was a passenger.

Homer and Langley Collyer
1947

Homer and Langley Collyer were compulsive hoarders. The reclusive brothers were found dead in their Harlem home, surrounded by more than a hundred and twenty tons of clutter they had accumulated for decades. Various items were guarded by booby traps set up by Langley to keep intruders away.

It is believed that he accidentally activated one of his traps while bringing food to Homer, who had lost his eyesight years before. Langley suffocated under a pile of debris, while his brother died of starvation and heart disease a few days later.

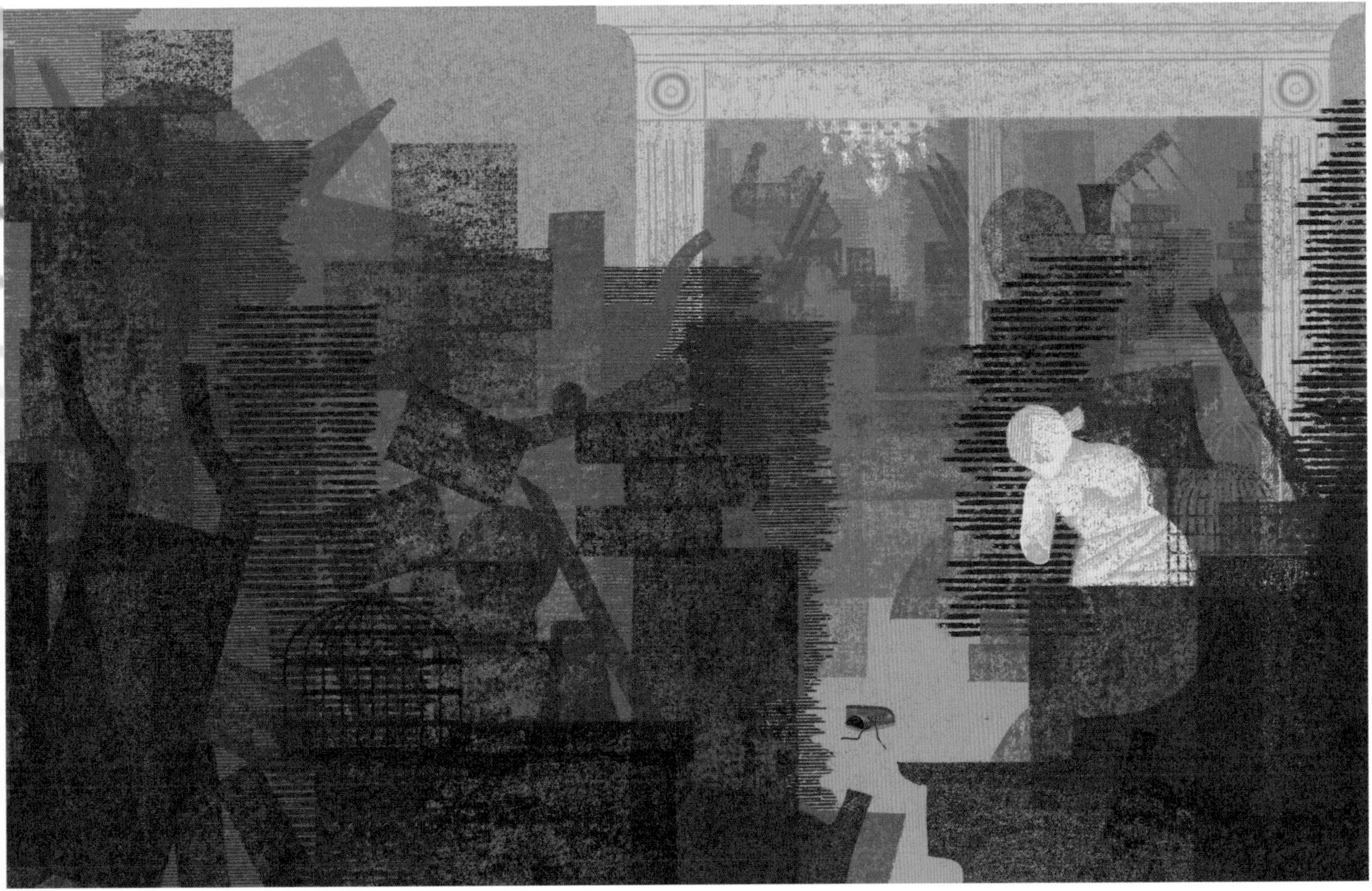

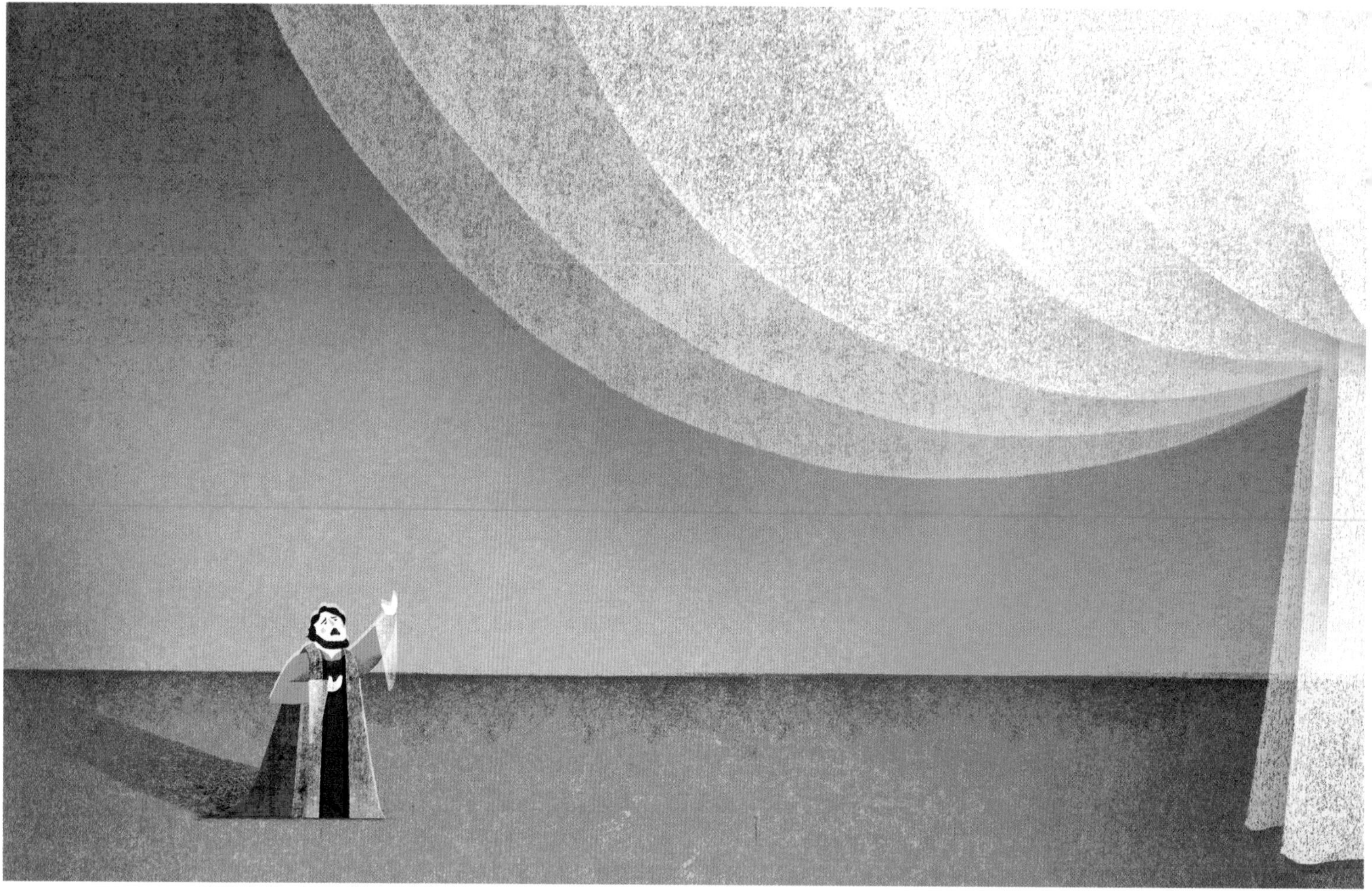

Leonard Warren
1960

Leonard Warren, a baritone at the New York Metropolitan Opera, died while performing the role of Don Carlo in *La Forza del Destino*. Warren suffered a massive heart attack as he began to sing the opening lines of his third-act aria, "Morir! Tremenda cosa!"— *To die, what a tremendous thing*.

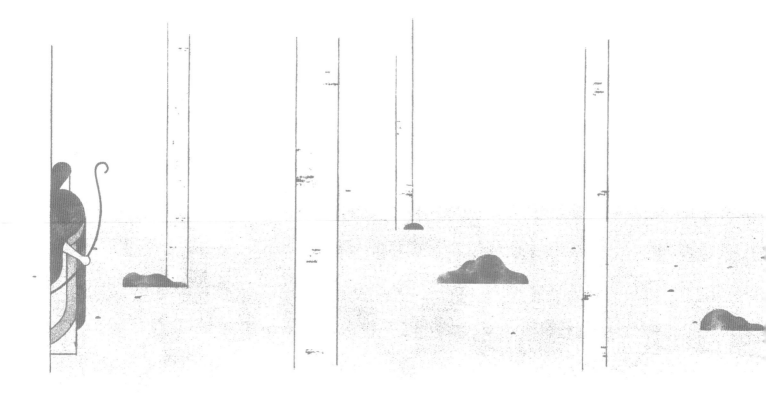

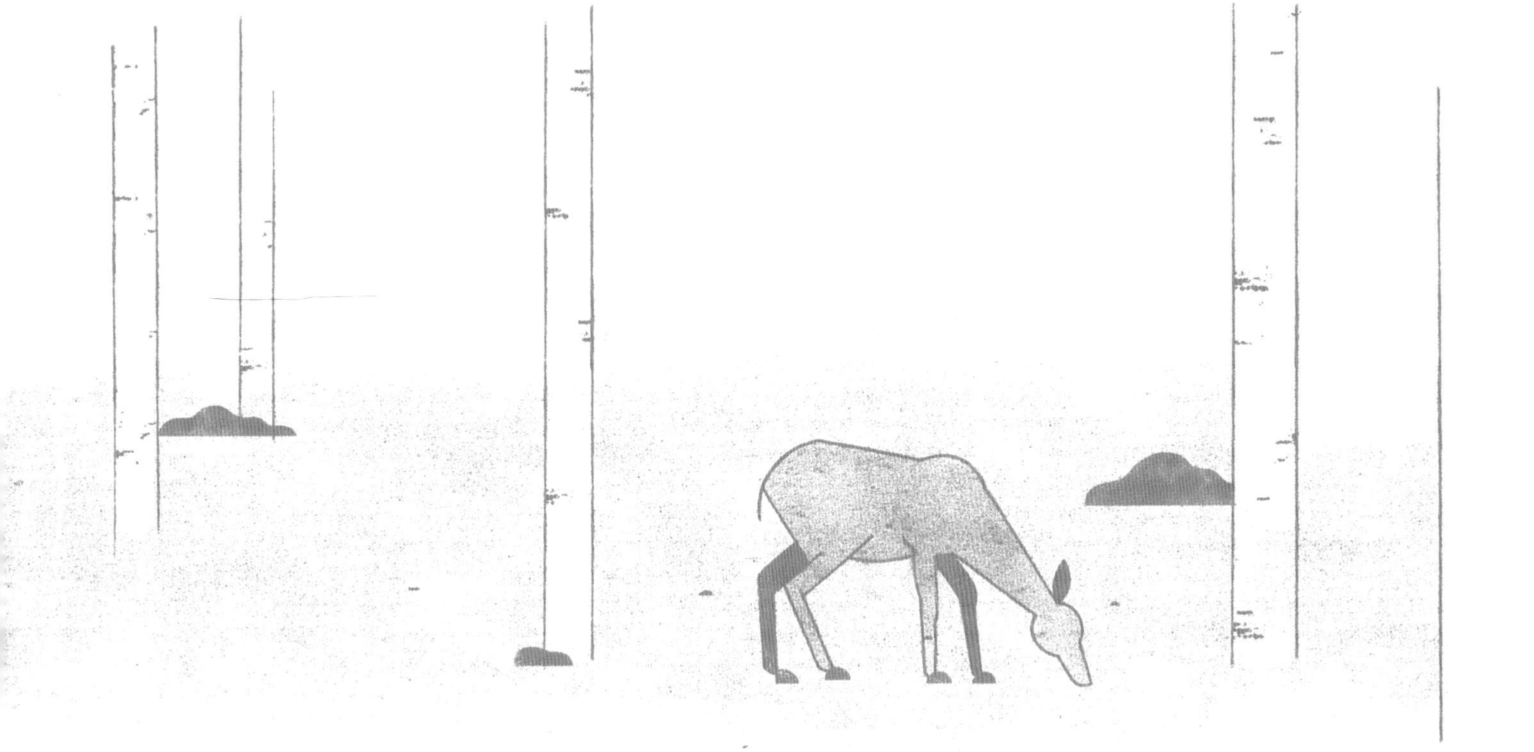

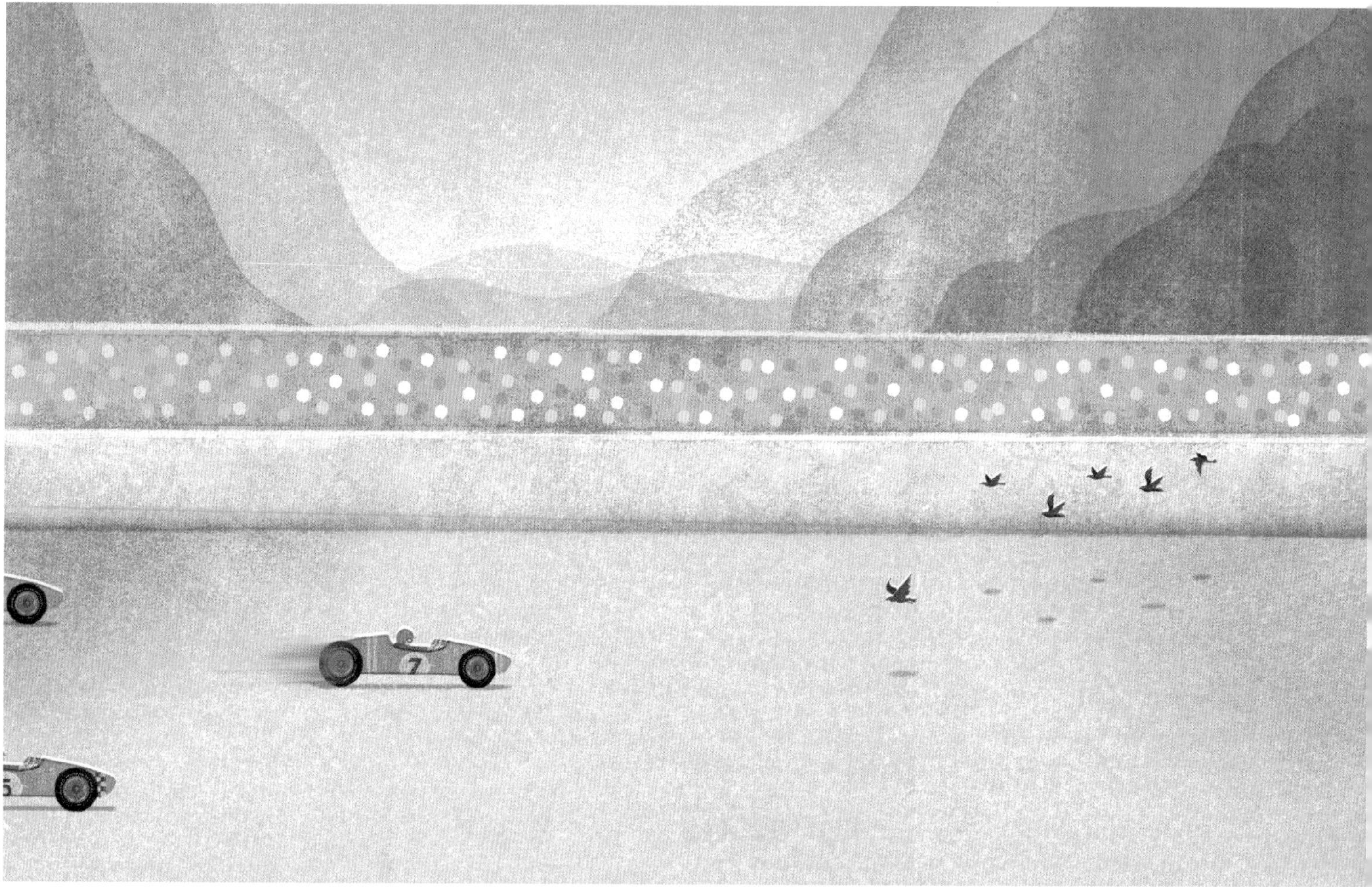
7

Alan Stacey
1960

Alan Stacey was a British Formula One driver who crashed and died during
the Belgian Grand Prix when a passing bird flew into his face.

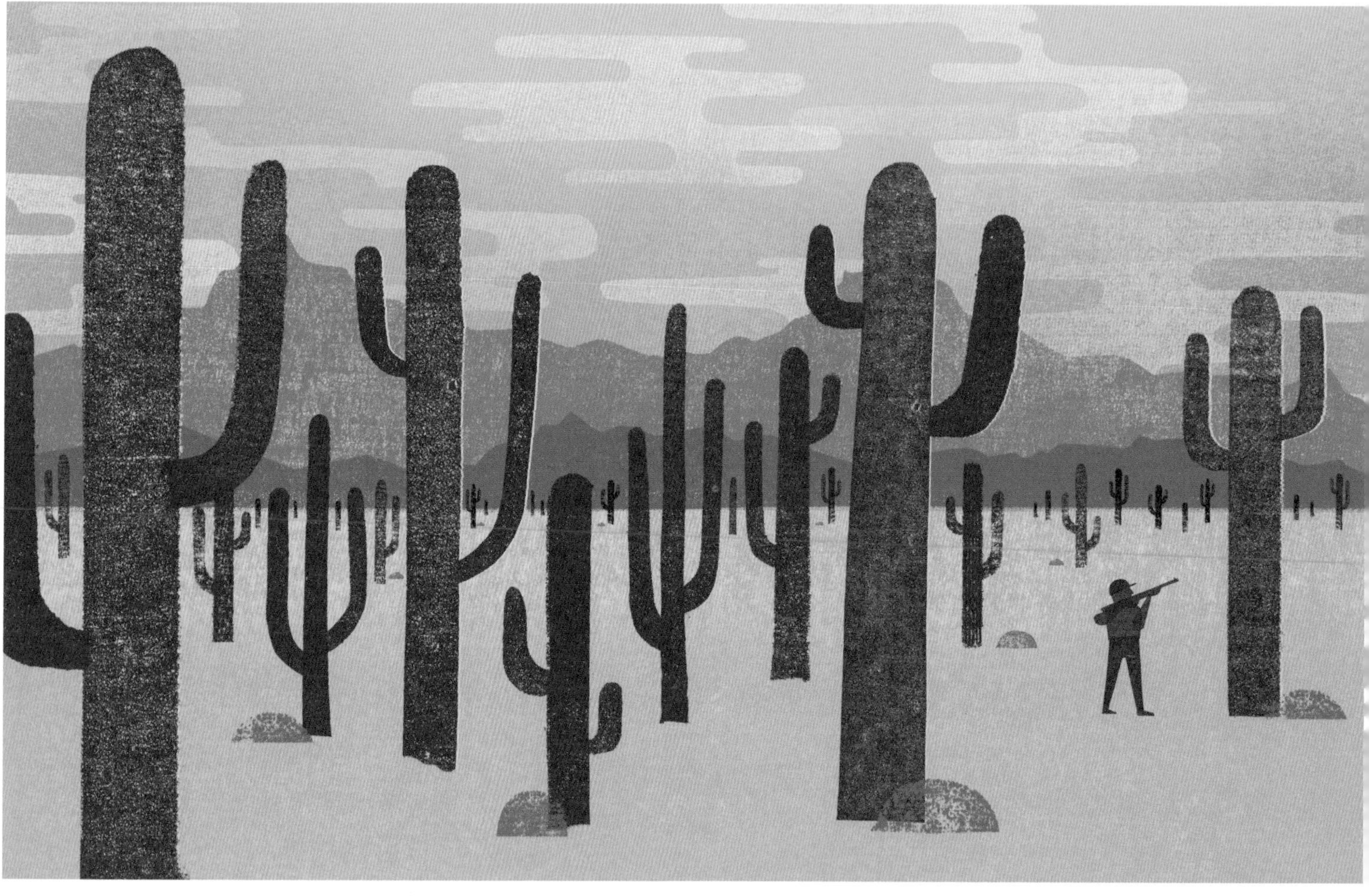

David Grundman
1982

David Grundman, a twenty-seven-year-old American, was killed by a plant.
After firing several shots at a twenty-six-foot-tall saguaro from extremely close range,
an arm of the cactus detached and crushed him to death.

Marc Bourjade
1982

Marc Bourjade was a French undertaker who died when a pile of coffins in his workshop fell on top of him. The coffin in which he was later buried was one of the ill-fated caskets.

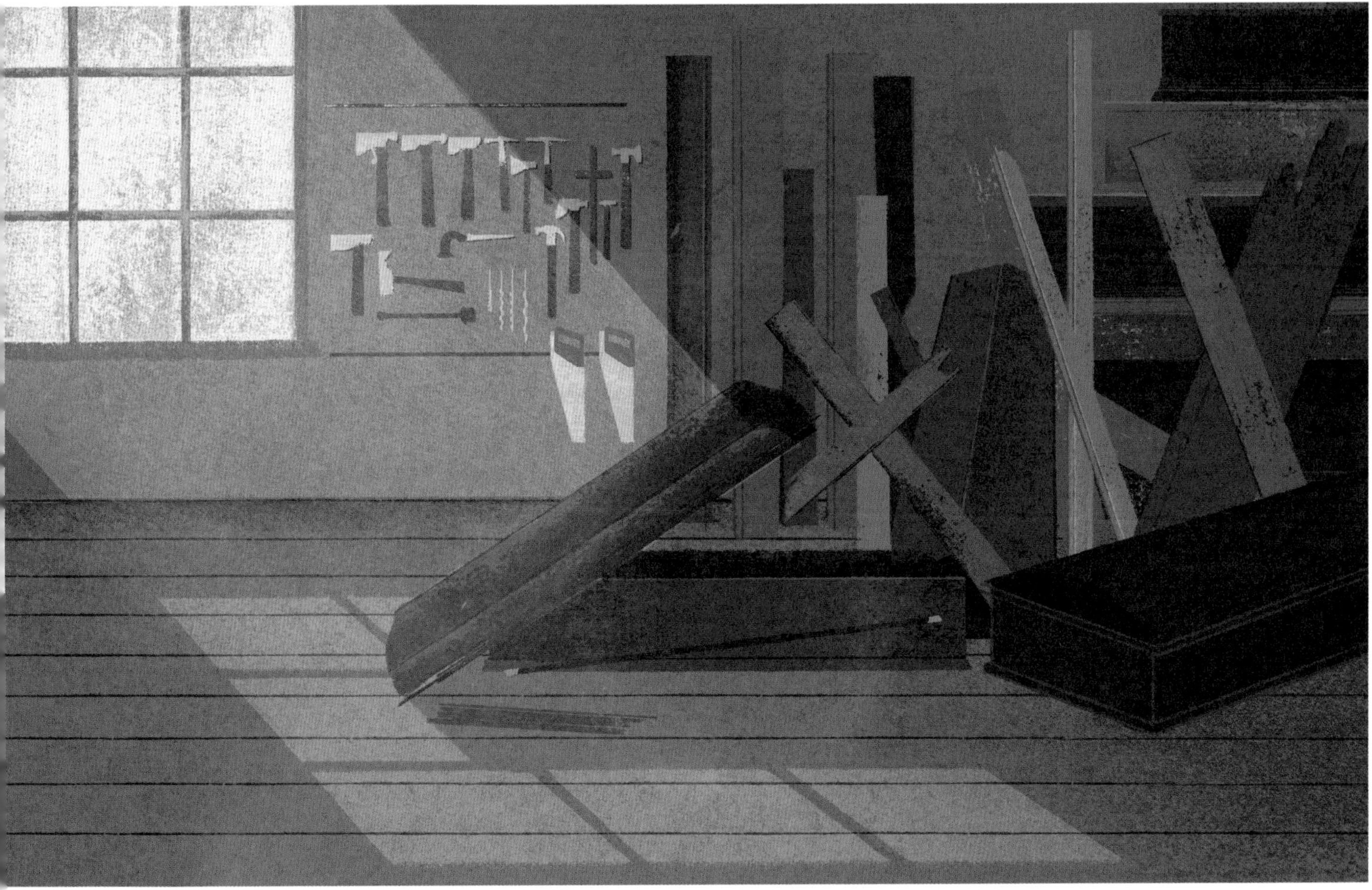

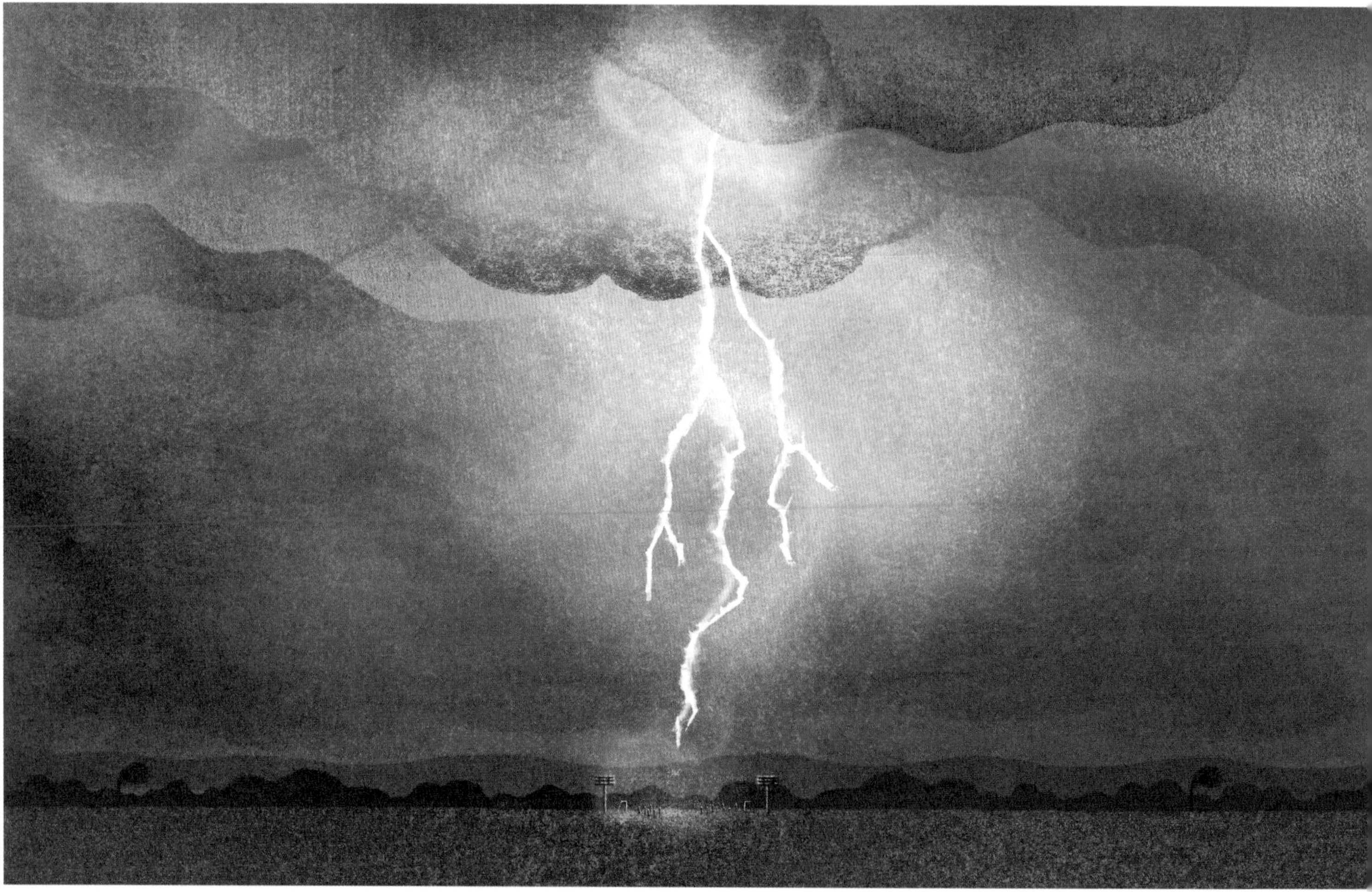

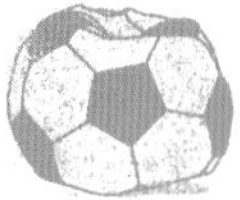

A Soccer Team

1998

An entire visiting soccer team was killed by lightning during a local match in the Democratic Republic of the Congo. Every single player on the opposing home team survived.

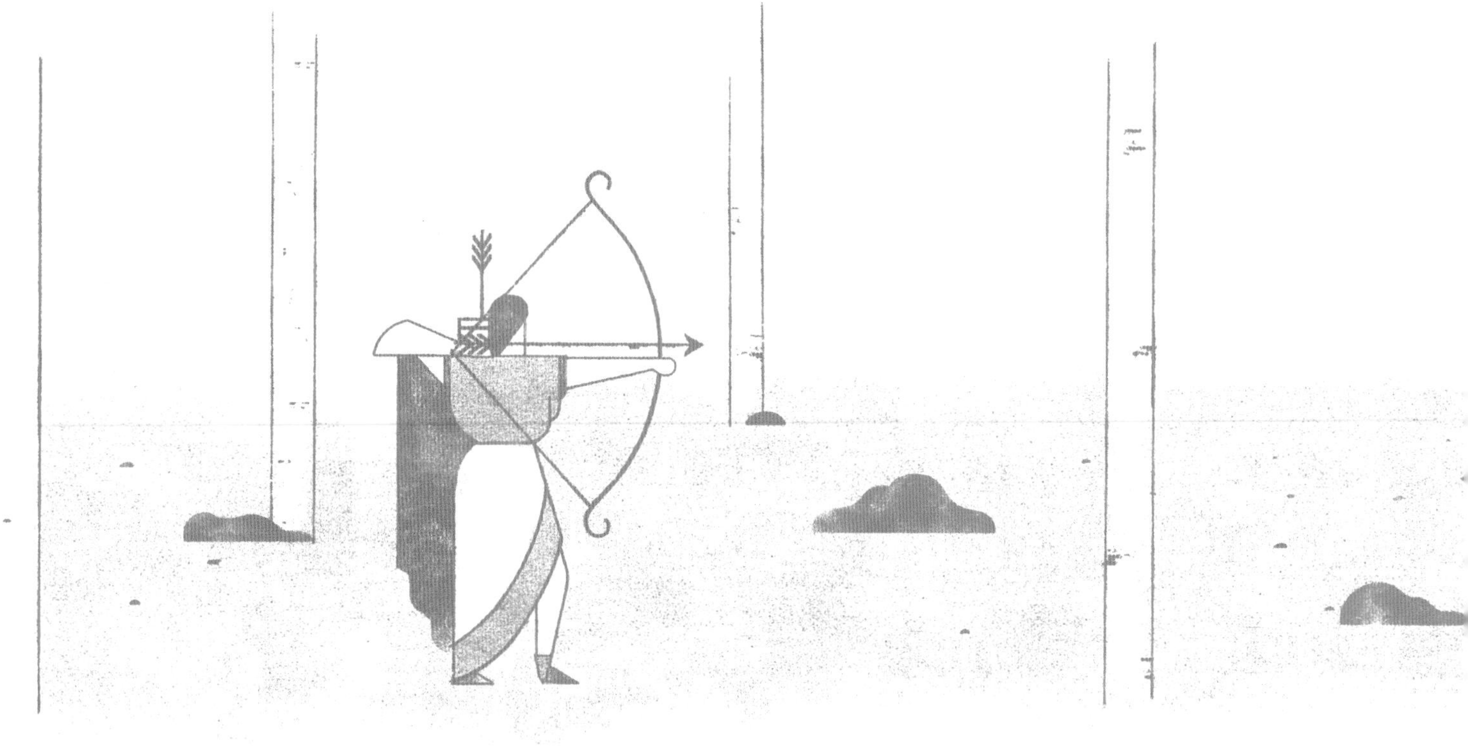

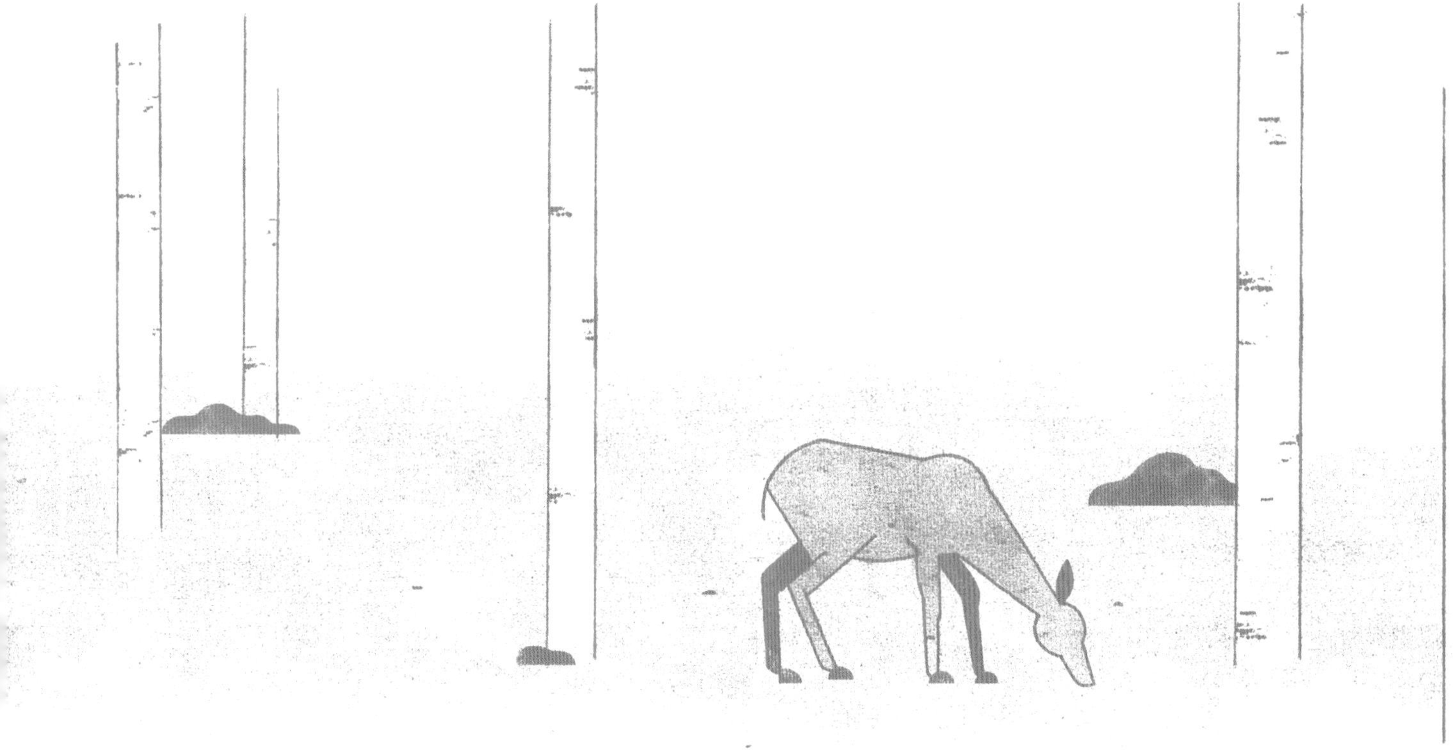

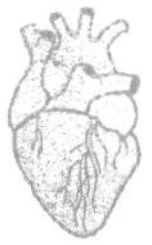

Sonny Graham
2008

Sonny Graham was a fifty-seven-year-old American who received the heart of a suicide victim, married the victim's widow, and around a decade later, died in the same way as his donor.

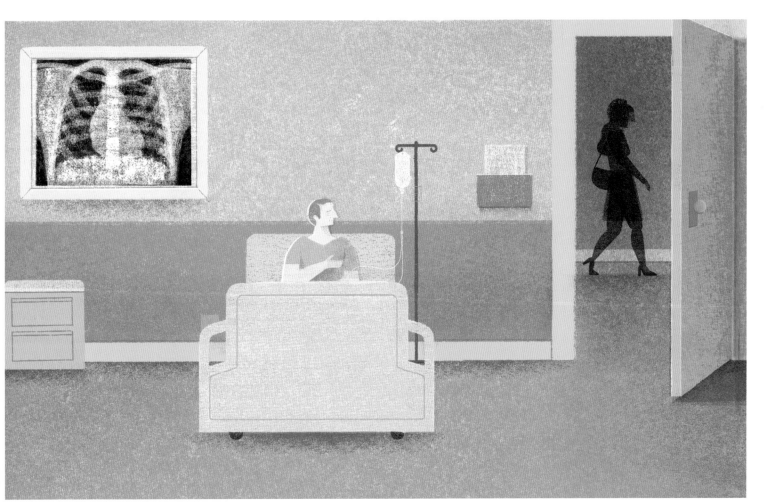

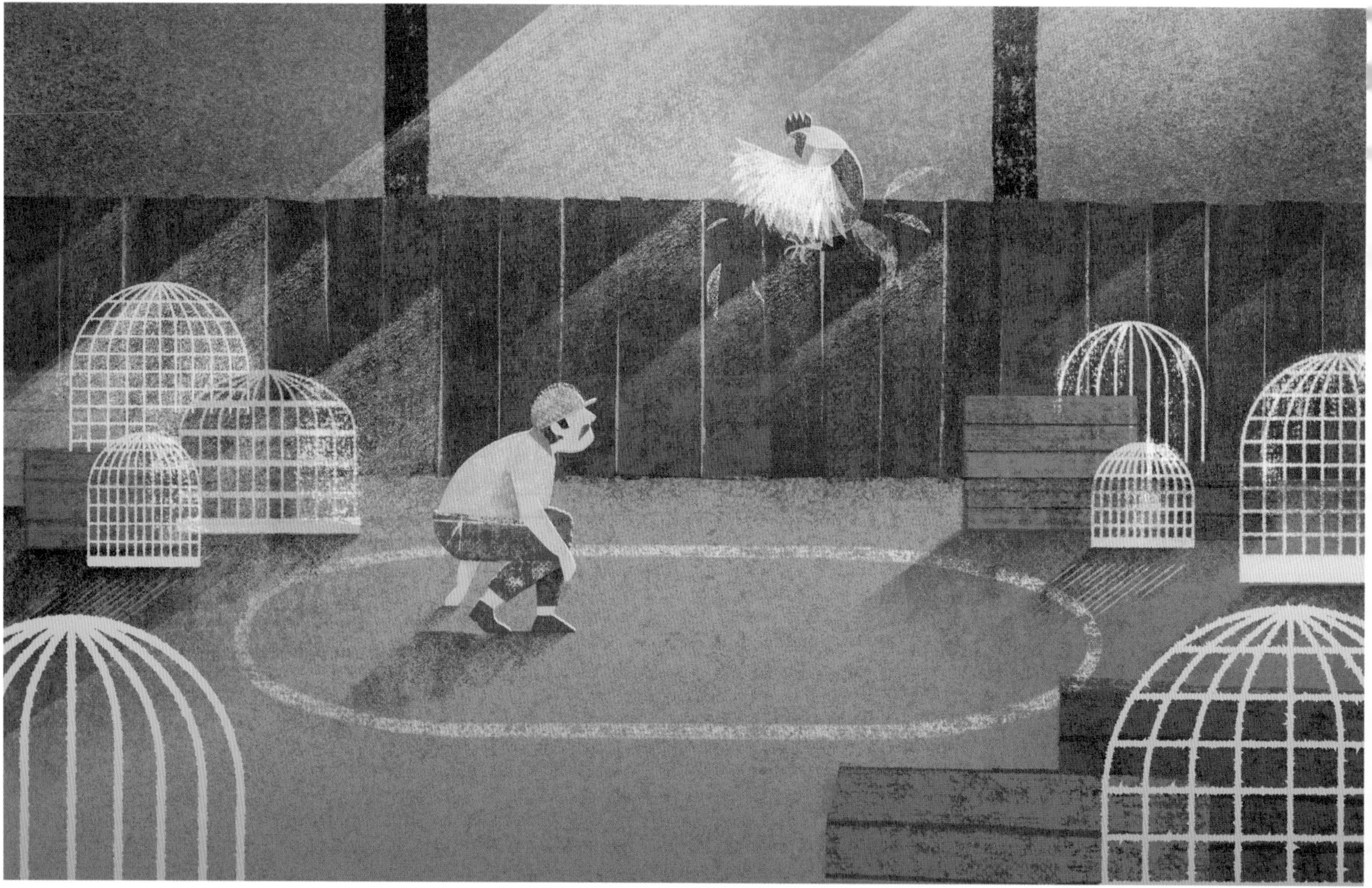

Jose Luis Ochoa
2011

Jose Luis Ochoa, a thirty-five-year-old man, was stabbed to death by
his own rooster during an illegal cockfighting match in Tulare County, California.

In cockfights, owners usually attach metal spurs to their birds' legs.
It was with one of these blades that Ochoa was killed.

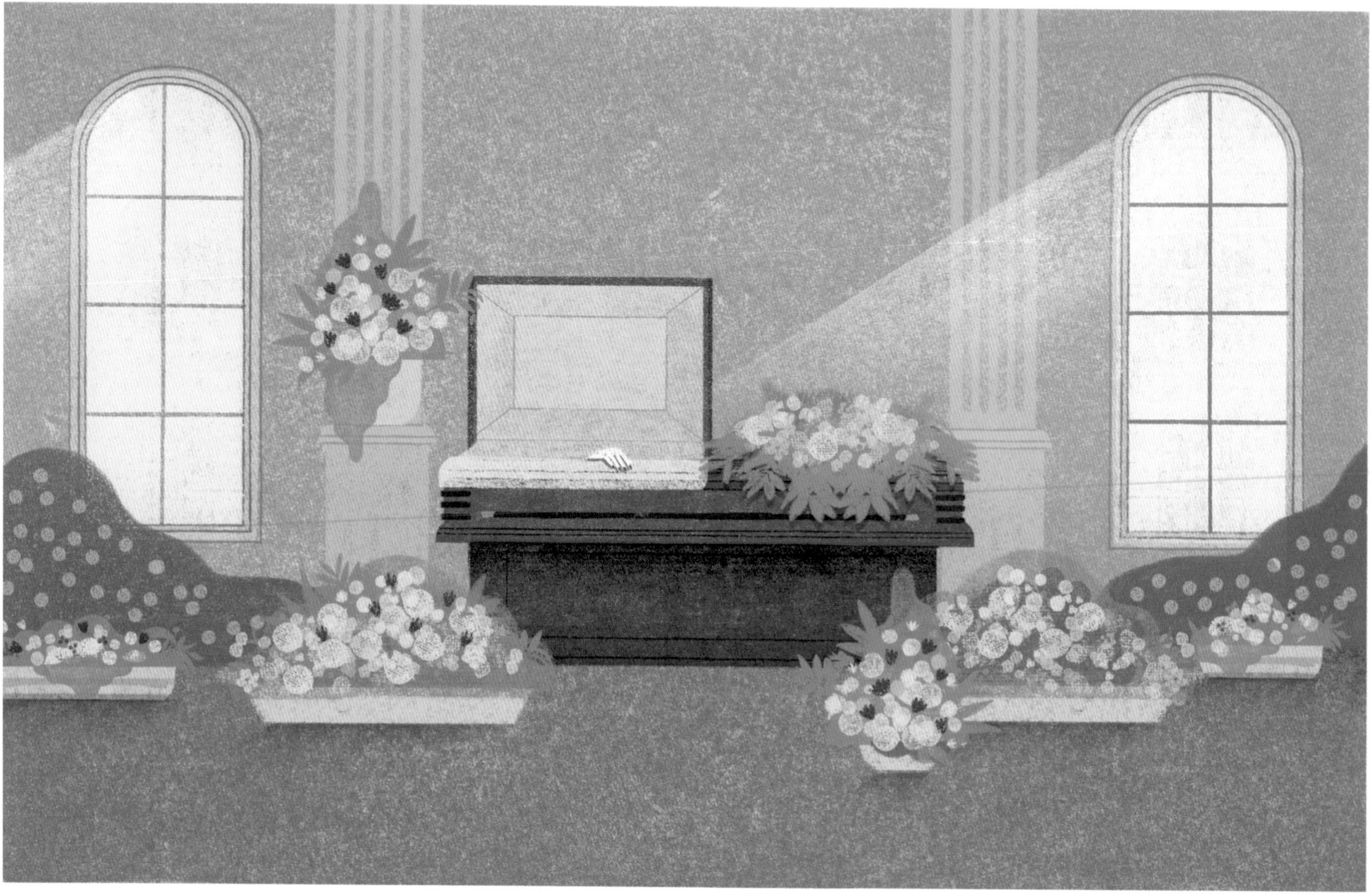

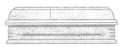

Fagilyu Mukhametzyanov

2011

Fagilyu Mukhametzyanov was a Russian woman who was mistakenly
declared dead by her doctors at age forty-nine. She died of a heart attack after waking
up at her own funeral, surrounded by grieving relatives.

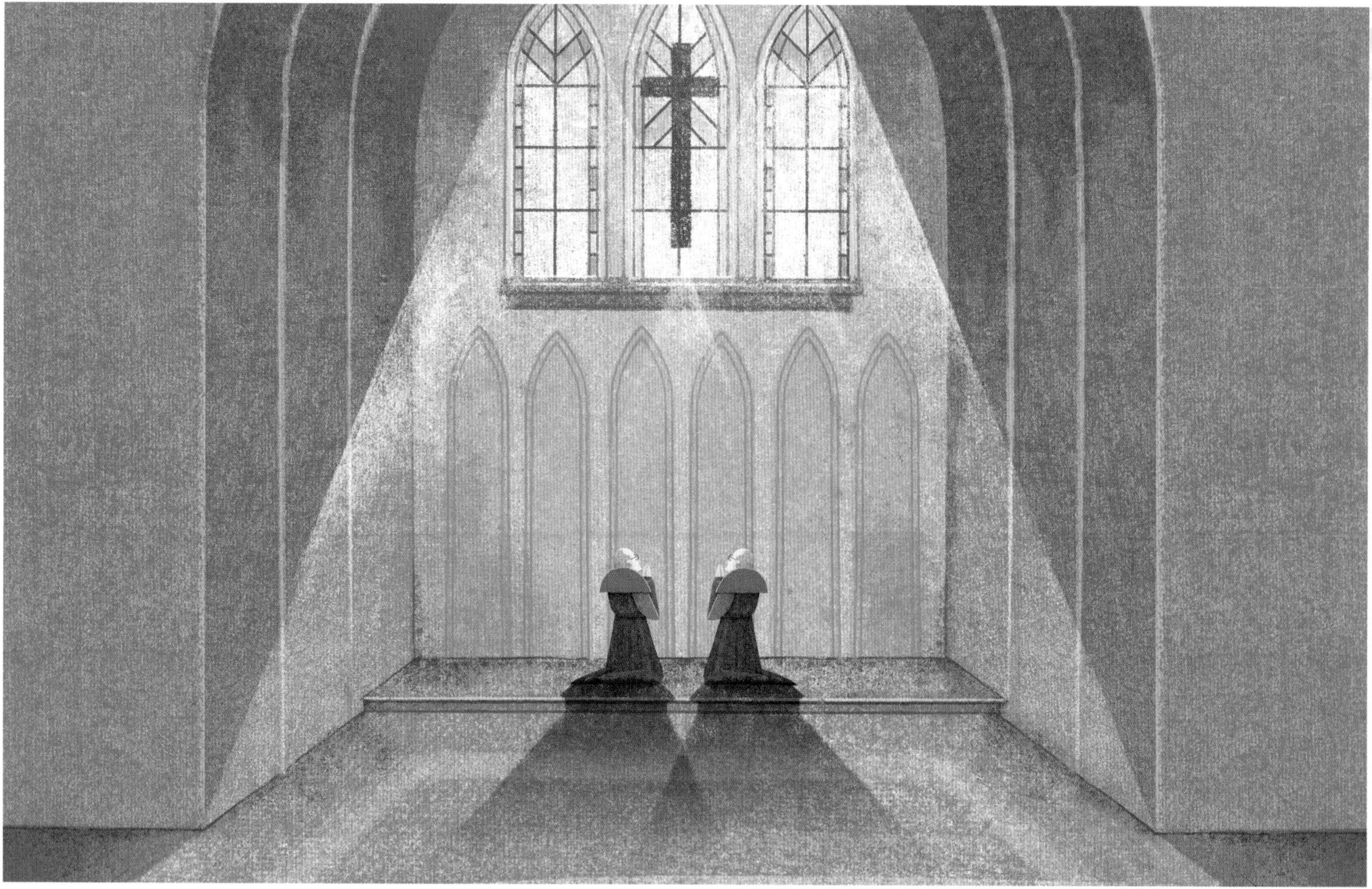

Julian and Adrian Riester
2011

Julian and Adrian Riester were identical twins who died identical deaths.
In their twenties, they had become Franciscan friars and lived together almost every day
of their lives. They died of heart failure in St. Petersburg, Florida, at age ninety-two.

For what is it to die but to stand naked in the wind and to melt into the sun?
And when the earth shall claim your limbs, then shall you truly dance.

—Kahlil Gibran